The
Picaresque
Novel

STUART MILLER

The Picaresque Novel

CLEVELAND AND LONDON

The Press of Case Western Reserve University

1967

FOR
Andrew Bongiorno
AND
Thomas McFarland

Acknowledgments

I owe warm thanks for help to many people who lived with me through the writing and various revisions of this book. René Wellek inspired my method—I could not have written my book without his generous advice. Lowry Nelson first introduced me to a rewarding subject. Among others, Peter Demetz and Henry Nash Smith offered me friendly criticism and encouragement. Joy Green Sweet, Roswell Angier, and Linda Thurston all provided indispensable editorial help as I worked through successive drafts. The University of California at Berkeley and the Research Council of Rutgers gave research monies that eased many burdens. Elinor Bacon gave me constant support through times when real and present obstacles seemed to blot any view of possible achievements.

I have dedicated this book to two of my undergraduate teachers who did their best to show me what was important in life and art. I owe them most of what wisdom the book may have.

Stuart Miller
State University College
Old Westbury, N. Y.
May 1967

Contents

Introduction

"... a certain kind of mind, called, perhaps a little too easily, the academic mind, insists upon exhaustive rites of classification."

—Irving Howe, *Politics and the Novel*

"... the literature of Rogues—dreariest of all."

—E. M. Forster, *Aspects of the Novel*

Introduction

ENRES, AS EVERYONE
knows, do not really exist. Croce has rightly told us that each
work of art is individual. Yet genre terms are inescapable if one is to
talk about literature. In fact, if one uses "genre" in a broad sense,
then one's first and fundamental descriptive and critical judgment of
a new work arises from his awareness of what *kind* of thing it is: we
pick up a mass of paper from the newsstand and say it is "a novel,"
"a comic book," "a newspaper," and so forth. We make genre
distinctions all the time, and they condition our understanding and
our evaluation of the work at hand. This being the case, our
problem is to define our genres with as much precision as we can:
otherwise, how can we know *what* we are talking about when we
use the distinctions? It is, of course, inevitable that any such attempt
at precision will run smash against Crocean truth: each work of art
is finally individual. And even the best genre definition will never
attain its goal; it will always describe an "ideal type," to use René
Wellek's phrase, not an empirical reality. Any attempt at genre
definition, therefore, is merely an essay; but we must make the
attempt if we are not to choose silence (Croce) or incoherence.

It is probably fair to say that the only literary genre which has
been treated at all well is tragedy. It may be that tragedy is relatively
easy to define, but more likely we should attribute the relative
coherence in our discussions of tragedy to Aristotle's having treated
the subject so early in the history of criticism. No one will say that
Aristotle had the last word on tragedy, but his *systematic* discussion

3

of the subject served as a model and a point of departure for all later criticism. The relative lack of clarity in discussions of comedy proves how much we have lost in not having had a clear and systematic foundation. Later genres like the novel elude definition still more, and the picaresque is no exception. Although the word "picaresque" has recently become popular in literary criticism, both professional and amateur, one would be hard pressed to find a really persuasive definition of the genre. There are studies of single aspects of the picaresque novel,[1] there are studies of separate picaresque novels,[2] and there are studies of the history (the variation from novel to novel) of the picaresque novel,[3] but there are no studies of *the* picaresque novel in the sense in which Aristotle's *Poetics* is a study of tragedy.[4] What is needed is a forthrightly systematic attempt to construct an "ideal genre type" for the picaresque novel showing how a number of coherent formal devices unite to produce a specific picaresque content and emotional response.

Such an attempt must be wide in its scope: if the picaresque is a genre, and it may not be, it must exist in examples that cross linguistic boundaries and occur over a long period of time. Any study of the genre as a genre must start with such a variety of examples and then elicit from them the common elements from which the ideal type can be constructed. But which examples? In order to avoid complete apriorism, we must use those novels which are generally agreed to be picaresque. *Tom Jones,* for example, has sometimes been called picaresque, but many a critic would hesitate to use this word for it—though the critic is usually not clear as to why he hesitates. The present study will try to make clear the reason for the hesitation by starting with works about which there is nearly universal agreement—and those works will be, first, the three great Spanish masterpieces, the originals of the genre: *Lazarillo de Tormes* (1554), *Guzmán de Alfarache* (1599 and 1605), and *El Buscón* (1626). To limit the point of departure to Spanish examples, however, would not satisfy the need for an international basis of definition. Accordingly, we will choose similarly "classic" examples of the picaresque from Germany (*Simplicissimus,* 1668), France (*Gil Blas,* 1715, 1724, 1735), and England (*The Unfortunate Traveller,* 1594; *Moll Flanders,* 1722; and *Roderick Random,* 1748). This international scope allows us also the chronological scope that we need. To find touchstones after the middle of the eighteenth century would be premature. It is generally agreed that the period from about 1550 to 1750 is the classic period of the picaresque; thereafter disagreement sets in as to what is picaresque and what is not. If we

4

are to define the genre systematically, we must define it in terms that more or less fit its classic examples before we go on to later works.

In making our definition we will have relatively little specific concern with history, whether literary or extra-literary. While one always needs historical knowledge in order to understand a particular literary work, our problem is essentially ahistorical. There are differences between *Lazarillo de Tormes* and *Guzmán,* differences also between *Simplicissimus* and *Moll Flanders.* These may be traced to certain historical changes outside the genre. One can show that *Lazarillo* is Renaissance in literary quality and *Guzmán* is Baroque. One can show that *Lazarillo* is the product of one epoch in Europe's *Geistesgeschichte* and *Guzmán* of another. One can even trace differences between two picaresque novels to socioeconomic changes. The secondary literature on the picaresque novel contains many efforts to establish the relationships between various picaresque novels and their diverse historical backgrounds. We must find, instead, what, if anything, is uniform in the novels that are called picaresque.

Part One

Plot, Pattern, and Rhythm

I will conclude this Chapter with telling thee; That when misfortune shall follow a man, no diligence, nor good counsell shall availe him; but shall, where hee thinks to gather wooll, goe away with his fleece shorne.

Man proposeth one thing, and God disposeth another. Who would ever have dream't, that things would have fallen out as they doe? What should one say unto it? There is now no helpe for it. For as a man cannot avoyde the stone, which a foole throwes by chance over a house, and kills him therewith: So, much less was it to be imagined . . . that such a businesse . . . should prove so disproportionable, and so quite opposite to our understanding.
—From Mabbe's translation of *Guzmán de Alfarache*

I

The Episodic Plot

HERE IS A MARKED
tendency, at least when the genre is not being handled with the
reverent hands of a specialist, to disparage the picaresque novel
because of its episodic plot. Such, for example, is the implication of a
distinction in Wellek and Warren's *Theory of Literature:* "In the
picaresque novel, the chronological sequence is all there is: this
happened and then that. . . . A more philosophic novel adds to
chronology the structure of causation."[1] This view of the episodic
plot is as old as Aristotle, and accounts for the usual scholarly view
of the picaresque novel as a type of primitive fiction which precedes
the triumphs of eighteenth and nineteenth century realism.

But there is no compelling reason to think of a causal plot as
more "philosophic" than a non-causal plot. In our intellectual climate, with its notions of uncertainty, the fragmentation of reality,
and the absurd, the older notions of order, predictability, and cause
and effect may not seem very philosophic (in the sense of true) at
all.* The episodic plot may reveal a chaotic lack of order in the
world and in ourselves and thus be more philosophic than the causal
plot. The philosophic import of the picaresque plot becomes clear
when it is contrasted with the plots of the "realistic" novel and the
romance.

The plot of the realistic novel is nothing more than an exhaustive
working out of Aristotle's plot of "necessary or probable sequence."

* The picaresque is by no means identical with the literature of the
absurd. See the "Conclusion."

The only difference, if there is any, is that the realistic plot is more probable than previous ones, since it attempts to be absolutely convincing according to the laws of probability. Ian Watt has shown the parallels between the devices of the rising realistic novel and the principles of modern science and philosophy.[2] He could easily have gone on to show how the devices of the new genre imply a world very similar to that of modern science and philosophy. The key concepts of this world are causal order, probability, and predictability. The realistic novel in its very plot structure expresses a world-view close to that of modern science and of modern everyday thought based on science. Character A does one thing which, perhaps only much later, is shown as affecting character B in a probable or "realistic" way. The reader's response to such a "model" realistic plot is an ordered response to an image of order.

The plot of the picaresque is, of course, totally different. The discrete fragments into which its events are broken express anything but order. The infinite possibilities of the picaresque plot express total openness. Since there are no limitations of probability, the door is left open to the fantastic, the improbable, and even the weird. The picaresque plot expresses an intuition that the world is without order, is chaotic.

The expressive function of a picaresque plot becomes still clearer when it is contrasted with another type of plot—the romance. The romance seems to have picaresque elements but is thought to be less realistic, e.g., *Daphnis and Chloe,* Sidney's *Arcadia,* Montemayor's *Diana,* and Heliodorus' *Aethiopica.* In the romance, cause and effect do operate, but the probability of their operation is more remote than in the realistic novel: there is an ordering of events, but it is not a *probable* ordering. The wonderful romance plot unravels a complicated pattern of chance and coincidence that works mysteriously toward some end. In reading such novels, one is surprised by a mysterious order which seems to exist in events. The reader's response to such a plot is awe. Rather than apprehending a world ordered by probable laws resembling those of modern science and psychology, he finds a world ordered by forces beyond his comprehension. The world order of the romance is that of inscrutable Fate and religion.

In the framed story of Ozmin and Daraxa that ends the First Book, Part I, of *Guzmán de Alfarache,* the typical romance plot centers around the eventual reuniting of the two Moorish lovers, who have been captured by the Spaniards. At the outset, the two protagonists seem made (by Fate?) for each other.[3] Daraxa's beauty is "the most perfect one, that ever eye had seene" (*1*, 164),[4] and she speaks "the purest Language" of Spanish (*1*, 165). Everything about her is perfect and therefore precisely defined. Ozmin's character is also definite and perfect: "Hee was young, rich, of a sweet behaviour, personable, discreet, and above all very valiant, and full of courage. . . ." He is "in all points sutable to . . . Daraxa" (*1*, 167).[5] The initial perfection of these characters suggests the total likelihood and desirability of a stable union between them. Mutually perfect, they love one another, and the fulfillment of their mutual perfections in union is what the heroes and readers hope to see. But life, with all its uncertainties, threatens to destroy this perfect union of perfect beings. There is a conflict in the romance between a social reality (often, as here, resembling the chaos of the picaresque world) and a sharply focused and stable affection between two perfect beings. The plot is then worked out by a series of wonderful events and coincidences, showing the ultimate victory of perfection over imperfection.

This plot has been described by Northrop Frye as one of the varieties of comedy's happy ending.[6] But the ending in the romance may also be tragic as, for example, in *Romeo and Juliet*. In either case, the world expressed by the plot pattern is a world controlled neither by chance nor probability, but by Fate. There seems to be a mysterious order in events that guides what at first looks like a set of chance occurrences toward some truly final end. If the realistic plot shows the operation of probability amid apparent disorder, the romance plot shows the triumph of Fate or Providence over the same apparent disorder.

We see this order working itself out in improbable incidents throughout Ozmin's and Daraxa's romance story, but at the end of the story the mysterious order emerges with particular brilliance. Apparently defeated at last by life's chaos, Ozmin is hauled into court on false charges. It begins to look as though the lawless picaresque world will win out in "the complaint of the Plaintifes; the accusation of Witnesses; the evill inclination of the Judges, (either upon information, or corruption; not favoring the Defendant,) besides the slaine and wounded (which were many)" (*1*, 227).[7] But the usual fortuitous coincidence occurs. While the hero is encompassed by dangers in a foreign land, his father and Daraxa's are captured by the Spanish and become Christians and loyal subjects of the Spanish crown. They are now in a position to help Ozmin, who is condemned to death. Immediately, "they . . . made their Majesties acquainted with the whole carriage of the businesse" (*1*, 229),[8] and

11

their Majesties quickly set all to rights.[9] At the last minute, Ozmin's execution is called off, the protagonists are married, and, we are assured, they live happily ever after.

The plot structure of the romance makes us see "how it all works out in the end." The chaos of stolen meetings, disguise, mischance, and frustration seems for a while to win out, but not finally. In the end, all these events are seen as having proved the constancy and virtue of the lovers and as having delayed any disaster until the fathers can be captured. The apparent misfortune of the fathers' being captured is the real good fortune of all. All become Christians and rich by their Majesties' patronage.

The pattern and meaning of the romance plot contrast absolutely with the episodic plot of the picaresque novel. In the picaresque, we start with life's chaos assaulting the picaresque hero in one event after another and we watch it continue to do so. Characters appear and disappear to no effect, forever forgotten. Usually the protagonist does not seek any stable relation between himself and another, as in the romance. If he does, he is usually frustrated. No mysterious order emerges to bind events together and to bring them to some end. In the picaresque plot viewed as a whole, nothing strictly speaking *happens*. The picaresque plot merely records fragmented happening after fragmented happening.

II

Some Specific Plots

O CLARIFY THE GENeralizations just made, a discussion of specific episodic plots is necessary. There seems little point, however, in giving summaries of the episodic plots of all our eight novels, since the notion that the picaresque novel typically has an episodic plot is widespread and correctly held. Instead, we will study examples of the picaresque novel in which the episodic plot combines with other patterns which may seem to (and sometimes do) modify the vision of disorder. My point will be that most of the major picaresque novels are episodic with a vengeance, and those countervailing plot patterns that we find do not substantially change the tone of the picaresque. They merely tease us with the hope of finding structure in the picaresque world. The "dance pattern" is the most important of these and must be defined before we can proceed.

It was noted above that characters appear and then disappear forever in the picaresque novel. In certain novels, however, they disappear and then, mysteriously, reappear without the picaro's seeking them. This mysterious and accidental reappearance of characters contrasts with reappearances in the realistic novel and, to some extent, in the romance. If this pattern occurs often enough in a novel, it is possible to see the protagonist as moving blindly through a complicated dance in which, at irregular intervals, he dances with a previous partner again, and again leaves him. This strange pattern may either soften or exaggerate the effect of chaos developed by the episodic plot and other devices. When it occurs frequently, we may not feel it as *ordering* the picaro's experience so much as limiting it. The possible combinations of his experience may seem fewer, and thus his life may appear somewhat more stable. This may seem especially true if the reunion results in some relatively long sequence of interaction with the person met. If, on the other hand, these re-encounters are rare, they may not significantly modify the totally open episodic plot. And if these remeetings are merely brief, one character quickly slipping from another, the dance pattern may emphasize the chaotic instability of things.

El Buscón is a good first example of both the episodic plot and other plot patterns. Pablos, the picaresque hero, begins in low, even underworld circumstances. He goes to boarding school, leaves, and then starts on the journey to the university at Alcalá. This is orderly so far, the character experiencing the order of growing up and the order he himself imposes on events by trying to rise in social station. When he is tricked on the road and in Alcalá, he decides to become a trickster himself, and from this point remains virtually unchanged by what befalls him. We do not have here the orderly development of character that is the forte of the realistic plot. Pablos acts and is acted upon, but no further substantial development takes place and the plot therefore seems random or disordered.[10]

The shift from milieu to milieu is another typical element of the episodic plot and enforces the sense of fragmentation and chaos. Instead of developing within a more or less closed group of characters as does the realistic novel's hero, the picaro constantly meets new characters and abandons old ones. Lazarillo, for example, recalls old masters, but never meets them again. Guzmán de Alfarache re-encounters only a handful of characters in that book full of characters. At home, he meets his mother again; he returns to Genoa to be revenged on his relatives; he also stumbles upon Sayavedra outside of Siena. But even from these reunions, however few, we get a sense of instability. His mother and relatives are quickly abandoned. Sayavedra is carried along only for a while and then kills himself. Such reappearances of characters as these are not likely to generate any sense of a stable order in events. In *El Buscón,* however, Pablos does re-encounter people continually, thereby making a dance pattern. But these people are often people we have never seen or heard of, like the "old friend who had been a student with me at Alcalá" (p. 219). In such cases as these, the author is merely economically managing his hero's introduction to a new milieu—here, the traveling players. The character met with is quickly forgotten for other members of the milieu, and no sense of a stable, constant social environment arises.

A dance pattern even more elaborate than that in *El Buscón* occurs in *Simplicissimus,* but it likewise gives no sense of stability, order, or direction to the episodic plot. At one point (p. 145) Simplicissimus has been captured by the Imperial forces and threatened with punishment for allegedly being a "traitor and enchanter" (p. 140). The Swedish forces suddenly attack, and who recaptures the down-and-out picaro but the young Herzbruder whom Simplicissimus had befriended at the siege of Magdeburg? Then (p. 132) Simplicissimus had been prosperous; now he is a wretched prisoner. Then Herzbruder had been driven out as a thief; now Herzbruder is an officer. The incident at first seems to show us only the vagaries of Fortune in the double-time of two separate careers. But whereas in a romance the two separate careers would both now become finally fortunate and the coincidence mark some providential order underlying life's accidental meetings, the reverse happens. Simplicissimus, it is true, is better off than before his capture but, almost in return for his success, the cosmic balance sheet haphazardly moves Herzbruder to the side of misfortune. Herzbruder is captured by the enemy almost immediately after freeing Simplicissimus. Coincidence here merely lets two separate fortunes brush each other briefly and pass their separate ways. No situation develops in an orderly way, and we are given the exact contrary of a sense of order and stability.

Later in the book, Herzbruder suddenly pops up at the place where Simplicissimus has been pressed into military service (p. 263). This time, the dance pattern results in good fortune for Simplicissimus without bringing down Herzbruder. But that good fortune, and that union of friends, is soon blasted by Simplicissimus' folly (p. 266). Here the coincidental meeting, though resulting in momentary stability through prosperous friendship, again serves only to emphasize the persistence of instability. Furthermore, the next sudden and coincidental reintroduction of Herzbruder emphasizes the chaotic change of events by showing the recently rich and successful officer thus: "there limped into the room a fellow with a stick in his hand, his head bound up, one arm in a sling, and clothes so poor that I would have given him not a penny for them" (p. 298).[11] In other words, the continual reconjunction of these two friends only contributes to the sense of fluctuating circumstance. Two careers are put in counterpointed rhythm to demonstrate the inability of two people to maintain a stable association. Finally, the randomness of inconsequential meeting emphasizes the very senselessness of life's structure.[12]

One more dance pattern meeting in *Simplicissimus* must be mentioned, since it further defines the difference between the role of coincidence in the picaresque novel and its role in romance and tragedy. One of the commonest and oldest plots in romance fiction has to do with a protagonist's late discovery of his true parentage. In the romance (e.g., *Daphnis and Chloe*) this discovery makes possible forbidden marriages between what seem to be different classes, or it brings prosperity to a deserving and long-suffering hero. In tragedy (e.g., *Oedipus Rex*) the hero discovers some dark pattern of coincidences that has made him violate taboos and has damned him. The reader feels an underlying providential order in the romance; he feels Fate and Destiny at work in the romance and tragedy.[13]

Late in *Simplicissimus,* the hero coincidentally meets his peasant foster father. We are prepared by our experience of romance and tragic plots for some great or decisive action to follow this wonderful coincidence. We are further prepared for some decisive ordering of past or future events when the foster father reveals *Simplicissimus'* true parentage. Since the tone of *Simplicissimus* is not tragic, we expect a reunion with powerful relatives and Simplicissmus' elevation to stable prosperity.

But Grimmelshausen is too much in control of his material suddenly to introduce a romance pattern into his picaresque world. He purposely disappoints our expectations by writing a dark parody of the romantic finale in which wonderful coincidence and *anagnorisis* are without significant consequence or issue whatever. The revelation has come too late. In their futility, accidental remeeting of foster father and *anagnorisis* of real parents are just so many more random events, emphasizing cosmic disorder rather than romantic or tragic order. Simplicissimus lamely reflects on his and our disappointment in finding no decisive resolution to his life in such wonderful discoveries:

> Now from that I knew clearly that I was the true-born son of my hermit and of Governor Ramsay's sister; but alas! far too late, for my parents were both dead, and of my uncle Ramsey could I learn nothing save that the Hanauers had rid themselves of him and his Swedish garrison, whereat he had gone crazy for rage and vexation [pp. 326-27].[14]

We have seen the episodic plot used in the picaresque to achieve the effect of chaos; moreover, we have seen the dance pattern introduced into the picaresque to emphasize, not attenuate, that effect. In *Gil Blas,* however, the new importance and quality of the dance pattern may make it different from other picaresque novels.

In earlier picaresque novels, the dance pattern occurred infrequently, offering brief but deceptive glimpses of order. In *Gil Blas,* however, scarcely a character is introduced who does not, more or less unexpectedly, turn up later. This controlling form gives the reader a definite sense of stability. Here the hero is seen moving in a peculiarly finite social universe with severely limited possibilities. He has a circle of friends and acquaintances that exists mysteriously around him, limiting his actions and bolstering his security. While we do not feel the hand of fate controlling these meetings and remeetings to some particular end (as in the romance plot), neither do we feel the lack of control and the limitation on action that characterize earlier picaresque plots.

When character after character disappears and reappears in *Gil Blas,* the reader is forced continually to remember earlier parts of the novel in order to place the reappearing character. The all-pervasive dance pattern forces the reader to pull the narrative together in his mind, much as a reader often is forced to see a poem as a pattern of images. Even so insignificant a character as the robber Captain Rolando appears twice (I, 1, iv; I, 3, ii). Gil Blas, who has left Rolando a robber, later finds him a constable. The reader remembers Rolando's last appearance, hears of his subsequent adventures, and is shown the pattern of Rolando's life stretching over some hundred odd pages of Gil Blas's own narrative. This picaro's story is held together by a filament of allusion and memory.

Often, the dance pattern is more elaborate than this, as in the continual reappearances of Laura (I, 3, iv; I, 3, ix; II, 7, vi; III, 12, i). Now it must be stressed that the remeetings and reappearances in the dance pattern are brought about by chance. When Gil Blas first meets Laura, she is pretending to be a great lady. Then, knowing she is a servant, he goes to see her and gets a job with her mistress. But when he next sees Laura, many pages later, it is by pure chance: he happens to go to a theater in Granada, and there she is. For a time he is her lover but then is put to flight. When, still later, Gil Blas is sent to look over a certain actress in Toledo, he discovers her to be Laura's daughter. Each time they meet, Laura brings Gil Blas up to date on what has happened to her, thereby unifying the otherwise episodic plot.[15]

The dance pattern, when fully developed as it is here, is of course similar to the pattern of the romance. The difference is that while in the romance a coincidence leads to some momentous conclusion, in the dance pattern it may lead to nothing more than a recitation of adventures or a job for the picaro. (It is largely the frequency of reappearances in *Gil Blas* that distinguishes its dance pattern from others.) The dance pattern thus stands between the typical picaresque and romance plots, giving a feeling of greater order in action than does the picaresque but less order than does the tightly fated design of the romance.

With the dance pattern moving the picaresque plot in *Gil Blas* toward romance, we should not be surprised to find actual romances included in *Gil Blas*. Romances like the story of Ozmin and Daraxa in *Guzmán de Alfarache* had already appeared in the picaresque tradition. But whereas in earlier novels these romances were set in frames so as to remove them from the picaresque world proper, in *Gil Blas* romance plot and world mingle easily with picaresque plot and world. That is, characters whose stories are romances appear in the picaresque plot alongside Gil Blas himself.[16]

For example, the tale of Donna Mencia (I, 1, xi, 55 ff.), the girl Gil Blas rescues from the robber cave, is a romance of love frustrated by the world and Fate (much like the Ozmin story in *Guzmán*). But here Donna Mencia mediates between the picaresque and romance worlds by her presence in both her own romance plot and in the basic picaresque one. The tale of Don Pomeyo de Castro is another example of the same thing (I, 3, vii), with its recounting of friendship's victory over love. Don Raphael's story has romance elements in it (II, 5, i), as do Don Roger de Rada's (III, 8, viii) and Don Gaston de Cogollos' (III, 9, vi; III, 11, xiii). The point in all these instances is that when the picaro encounters a romance character in his own world, the romance and picaresque worlds become subtly fused.

Because the most prominent example of this mingling is Don Alphonso's tale, it is worth analyzing in some detail. Gil Blas encounters Don Alphonso by chance (II, 4, ix, 96). Since Gil recognizes him as the man described by the police as a fugitive from justice (II, 4, ix, 95), Alphonso tells him his romantic tale with its burden of wonderful coincidence (II, 4, x, 99 ff.). Alphonso is an orphan brought up by a certain Baron Steinbach in Madrid. He has engaged in a fight with an unknown man over a girl and killed him. When he fled, there was a storm, and he took refuge in a house. He met there a girl, Seraphina, with whom he promptly fell in love, but the hand of fate had been managing the romance plot, for the girl was the sister of the very man Alphonso had just killed. Don Alphonso fled again in despair.

At this point, Alphonso's narrative approaches the book's own narrative present; we have been brought up to date. Now comes the digression of Don Raphael's tale (II, 5, i), which brings Don Raphael's semipicaresque and semiromantic history up to the present. At last, the picaresque action proper may proceed again, except that it is not a picaresque action which follows, but a romance one. When Raphael, Ambrose, Alphonso, and Gil Blas rescue a man and woman held by some robbers, who should the pair be but Don Alphonso's beloved and her father? The romance plot moves toward its wonderful resolution with Alphonso having (1) unknowingly murdered his beloved-to-be's brother and (2) unknowingly rescued his beloved and her father from murder.

The mingling of romance and picaresque pattern continues until romantic destiny contrives to have Alphonso forgiven by Seraphina's father. All barriers of law and family hatred suddenly removed, Alphonso and Seraphina are married and no doubt live happily ever after. And Gil Blas, the picaro, is both participant in, and witness to, these romance events.

The next example of the picaresque (*Moll Flanders,* 1722) reverts to the episodic plot of earlier novels. It is clear now that the plot of *Gil Blas* differs in kind from the plots of the other books we call classic picaresque novels. In the first part of *Moll Flanders,* the heroine runs through husband after husband; in the second, she runs through trick and theft after trick and theft. The husbands and tricks are, by and large, distinct from one another. There is no dance pattern and no mingling of picaresque and romance plots. Instead, eighteenth-century England gives us almost as chaotic and episodic a plot and world as seventeenth-century Spain or the Germany of the Thirty Years War was able to produce.[17]

There are differences, however, between the purely episodic plot and the plot of *Moll Flanders*. The accident of Moll's marrying her own brother smacks heavily of the romance or tragic plot of fate. But this "most unexpected and surprising thing that perhaps ever befell any family in the world" (p. 101) is robbed of any great sense of destiny because it leads to nothing final. The discovery has grave emotional effects on all concerned but neither ends the action nor gives it decisive direction. Moll simply goes on from husband to husband as before.

Another pattern that might distinguish the plot of *Moll Flanders* from a purely episodic one is the appearance of certain characters through sizable sections of the narrative. To take a prominent example, Moll's "governess" figures in more than half the book. We might expect this pattern to weaken the sense of discrete separation of events that we found in such a book as *El Buscón*. But even though Moll Flanders lives with her governess during the whole time of her thievery, each thieving episode is distinct, happening in a different place, among different people and, thanks to her disguises, often to a seemingly different character. The episodic plot still dominates the novel.

Roderick Random exhibits all the episodic character of the earlier picaresque novel but also employs a dance pattern which partially modifies that character. As to the book's episodic nature, it is commonly objected that no man could have experienced in a lifetime the adventures that Roderick experiences from his teens to his late twenties. We may agree, provided we do not view the packing of disconnected events as a flaw. The stunning accumulation of Roderick's adventures magnificently projects feelings of impermanence and instability.[18]

We may conclude this despite the presence of a dance pattern in the novel, a dance pattern probably directly inherited from *Gil Blas,* which Smollett admits he imitated in *Roderick Random.*[19] In *Gil Blas,* the dance pattern was part of a new "classicizing" or ordering of the picaresque, but in *Roderick Random* it does not substantially affect the book's picaresque character because of its infrequency and casualness. Like Gil Blas, Roderick Random meets and remeets many characters: Beau Jackson, Miss Williams, Thomson, Gawky, Strap, and Bowling are examples. But the dance pattern here is not usually connected with any plot development. He leaves Strap, his companion, in London and bumps into him years later in France. He leaves his sponsor Lieutenant Bowling in Scotland and finds him again in France. But there is no evident order to these meetings. Strap has been fortunate and can help Roderick when he remeets him. Bowling has been unfortunate and cannot. Other factors that prevent the dance pattern from ordering this book as it did *Gil Blas* are the heightening of the Fortune pattern, motifs such as violence and the lack of law and order, and the emphasis on the "rush of events."

III

Rhythm

PICARESQUE DEVICE
closely related to the episodic plot is the piling of event on event in
strikingly short compass. Such rapid action sequences are very frequent in the picaresque novel and have the effect of dazzling both
reader and picaro with the accumulated chaos of life's action.
Guzmán de Alfarache presents many examples of this rhythm of
rapid action. Early in the first volume of Mabbe's edition, Guzmán
calls our attention to the rush of events by summing up the story to
follow thus:

> They [troubles] began now to come fast upon me, and followed
> me at an inch, not allowing me one moment of content, nor
> affoording mee so much as a breathing-time from my cares, all
> the while that I was abroad in my travels . . . [1, 97].[20]

But the actual events we are shown in the first volume of the
Mabbe translation do not quite give us the *feel* of this machine-gun
assault by experience. It would seem that Alemán only gradually
came to realize the expressive power of the rapid action pattern,
and when he did come to use it, he used it structurally, to underscore
the tenuousness of man's stability.

Guzmán has been comfortably employed by a cook, but three
sudden accidents (Guzmán bumping into the cook's undressed wife,
Guzmán discovered stealing eggs, Guzmán discovered trying to sell
a stolen shank) shatter his stability and move him and the plot on in

a great rush (2, 22-60). Now the larger incident itself, i.e., the forty-page account of the time spent at the cook's, has been digressive, more concerned with *describing* the way of the world or Guzmán's general activities than in *dramatizing* particular events belonging to the plot or action per se. Guzmán has described, for example, the roguish manners of cooks (2, 49-51) and their thefts, the corruption of the rich man's household (2, 44-49), the vanity of human wishes (2, 39 ff.), and so on and so forth. This pattern is to become important in *Guzmán* and other picaresque novels: digressive, descriptive rambling about whatever comes to mind, usually directed at exposing a corrupt world in all its facets, is punctuated by a rush of events.

Often the rush is generated by a combination of the world's malice and the almost metaphysically chaotic force of events themselves. We see such a pattern beginning when Guzmán courts Fabia, a Roman lady, on behalf of his master, the French ambassador. Confident of success because of the assurances of Fabia's maid, he goes to Fabia's house for a long-sought interview. The outcome of this expectation is surprising and even shocking. Horrible brutality and bewildering rhythm are structurally combined when the series of tricks and accidents Guzmán endures becomes progressively more rapid and brutal. It begins when Guzmán is tricked into waiting all night outside Fabia's house in a driving rain, the mud rising around his ankles, expecting an interview that does not occur. At last, Fabia talks with him for a moment, making some excuse for the delay. But cheer changes to despair as Fabia tells him to take shelter in a court. It is, of course, a hog sty, full of dung. Moreover, still in the rain, Guzmán finds himself locked in the sty. Finding a way out at last, he returns home mortified and shaken, but comes back the next night at Nicoleta's request. As he is explaining to the likewise duped Nicoleta what treachery he has undergone, one of those startling and perverse picaresque accidents occurs. A mad boar appears out of nowhere and runs between Guzmán's legs. Backward astride the hog's back, Guzmán is carried away. When he is flung into the dirt and finally pulls his filthy body up, he is mocked by people from their windows until he is like "one that was out of his wits" (3, 119).[21] The rapid onslaught of another's trickery and the world's cosmic perversity in driving a man out of his wits will become a common picaresque sequence. The effect of this rush of events is felt by the reader as well as the picaro because of the first-person point of view.[22]

But Guzmán's trials are not done—the mad rush of events is not yet over. He takes refuge for a minute in a house, but when he is turned out, the passersby mock him again (*3*, 123). Even the dogs follow him and nip at his calves (*3*, 124), until he finds momentary rest at home. All these events occur in the bare space of fifteen pages in the Mabbe translation (*3*, 111-25). The crowd and dog psychology are probable, but the lumping together of so many comic persecutions is not "realistic," not an imitation, but an expression of the dizzying rush of human experience and, in particular, misfortune. The effect on the picaro, standing at last at his master's gate (*3*, 126), his key lost, is again madness: "With these exclamations [of despair] (wretched as I was) I rent the ayre, and was ready to runne out of my wits." [23]

What has been related is only the beginning of a blinding series of misfortunes for Guzmán. In the succeeding pages, though they are punctuated by many digressions and the rhythm is somewhat moderated, the same dizzying rush of events continues. Forced to leave Rome out of shame over the foregoing incidents, Guzmán is befriended by a Spaniard who turns out to be a thief and a deceiver, and is turned out of doors by another supposed friend. The cycle of bad events is broken momentarily by a reunion with one of them, but it picks up again when Guzmán is clapped into jail by a corrupt judge and robbed of his money. The innocent comic punishment of Guzmán the bawd, begun so many pages earlier, has finished with a rush of every kind of disaster. A night in the rain has ended in the corruption of friendship and justice. Improbable link after improbable link has fashioned a typical picaresque rush of events, but the rush-of-events rhythm is structurally employed. This uneven chain of events has more links at the beginning than at the end. A blistering rush of event and accident introduces a more paced assault of circumstance to the picaro and through him to the reader.

The chaotic nature of this world is amplified by the picaro's own mode of living, by the innumerable tricks he plays on others. If the rush of events already described usually consists of an assault by other people and by circumstance on the picaro, his own dazzling series of tricks is a vengeance on reality for just that assault. The rapid series of tricks, then, has two effects: (1) It enforces the impression of the rush of action in life; the reader is given just so many more disorganized actions in a short space. (2) It demonstrates the picaro's capitulation to his chaotic world. *Lazarillo*, for example, begins with a rapid series of tricks. When the blind man tricks him with a stone bull, Lazarillo retaliates in the short compass of the first chapter with the food bag trick, the trick of putting alms in his mouth, the trick of the hole in the bottom of the wine jug, the grape trick, the sausage trick, and so forth. The first picaresque novel is stuffed full of the rapid, jagged play of events expressed as trickery. In *Lazarillo,* of course, trickery becomes the norm of existence and so the trickery motif has special meaning. To live, Lazarillo learns, one *must* be a rogue.

In *The Unfortunate Traveller* this insight appears from the beginning, since the book opens with an even more disconnected barrage of trick events than does *Lazarillo.* Jack tricks a cider merchant (pp. 204-10), sends off a leeching captain as a spy (pp. 210-17), quickens the pace with a one-paragraph narrative of how he disguised himself as a whore to get money from a "Switzer Captain" (p. 217), and breathlessly adds how he cheated some stingy, dishonest clerks (p. 217). The effect is more jagged than that in *Lazarillo* and more rapid.

In *Guzmán de Alfarache,* however, the rapid series of tricks has greater structural significance. After his elaborate swindle of a merchant in Milan (Second Part, Second Book, Chs. vi-vii, Mabbe, Vol. 3), Guzmán is primed to wreak havoc in Genoa. He has recovered from the fall that began in Rome, and as a full-fledged trickster now, wreak havoc he does. In a single chapter he pulls off no less than four separate and elaborate tricks (Second Part, Second Book, Ch. ix, Mabbe, Vol. 3). He revenges himself on his uncle and other relatives (who mistreated him in an earlier visit) by getting them to give him jewels and clothes on the security of trunks full of stones. He beguiles a cousin into lending him six hundred crowns on the security of a gold-plated lead chain. He and Sayavedra cheat some gentlemen gamblers at cards to the tune of 15,000 royals. And to top it all off, he stealthily leaves his innkeeper trunks full of rubbish as pay for his lodgings. This rapid sequence of tricks corresponds structurally to the rapid sequence of misfortunes beginning in Rome. The specific revenge on his relatives for their mistreatment in the first part is also felt by the reader as a generalized revenge on experience for its mistreatment of the picaro at Rome and thereafter.

The same symmetrical use of the trick pattern occurs in *El Buscón,* Chapter Five. The whole chapter covers seven pages in English translation (pp. 110-17) and describes only one day, but an event-filled day it is. In it the picaro (not yet a picaro) is assaulted by trick after trick: the initiation fee, the students' pretending that Pablos smells, Pablos spat upon, Pablos beaten by the innkeeper, Pablos beaten by Don Diego (pp. 112-13). At this point, Pablos remarks with typical hard-earned picaresque philosophy, "But when misfortunes begin, there is no end to them, for they are linked each to each, and the one that comes first inevitably drags the others after it" (p. 113).[24] And so Pablos is whipped in bed and assaulted with excrement. At the end, Pablos points toward the picaresque rhythm by saying: "When I was alone, I could not help observing that more, almost, had happened to me that one day in Alcalá than had happened to me the whole time I stayed at the Goat's" (p. 116).[25] The barrage of incident has convinced him that it is representative of adult experience, and Pablos retaliates with a counterbarrage in a rapid series of tricks immediately following.

As in other picaresque novels, the rhythm of events in *Simplicissimus* is used with structural cunning. The rhythm gets increasingly rapid toward the end. The picaro's own summary of *one* year's events (i.e., from his second marriage to the time when he is first told of the Mummelsee) indicates how fast events move, if we remember that a bare twelve pages (320-32) in the English translation are sufficient to contain them:

> I . . . pondered on the changes I had suffered since then. I represented to myself how in that very place I had begun to be in place of a free man a slave of love, and how since then I had become from an officer a peasant, from a rich peasant a poor nobleman, from a Simplicissimus a Melchior, from a widower a husband, from a husband a cuckold, and from a cuckold a widower again; moreover, from a peasant's brat I had proved to be the son of a good soldier, and yet again the son of my old dad [p. 332].[26]

But the pages that relate such a rush of events are by no means the most action-packed in the book. Those occur even closer to the end, in the detailing of Simplicissimus' wanderings from Russia throughout half the world (pp. 353-54). In these wanderings we are told in a brief space how he is captured by Tartars, sold to China, given to the King of Korea, let go to travel homeward through Japan and Macao, taken through the East Indies for a year by Turkish corsairs, sold to Turkish merchants in Egypt, taken as a galley slave to Turkey, and freed at last by the Venetians.

The increasing tempo of events is strategic in preparing the original ending of the novel. Just as his earlier buffetings by the world in the beginning had hardened the innocent boy into trickster and marauder (pp. 1-151), so these final rushes of events also have a decisive, if contrary, influence on him. Both sequences are taken by the hero as typical of life's experiences, but the later rush of events is too much for him. Instead of deciding to react against life's chaotic assault as picaresque assaulter, he decides to leave the chaos altogether and become a hermit. This final decision seems valid and plausible in large part because of the rapid rhythm of action at the end. In this barrage of events we readers are made to feel the disorder of the world in quintessential form. Like the hero, we too are bombarded (through his point of view) with incidents, and because of the short compass of our reading time, the barrage effect is even enhanced. Who would not forsake such rushing bewilderment?

Rush-of-event patterns like those described appear in *Gil Blas*, but on the whole their rhythm is muted. The slowing down of event in this novel contributes to the sense of a more stable world than we find in other picaresques; the effect is the same as that achieved through the dance pattern and the mingling of romance and picaresque plots. The fastest sequence of events in *Gil Blas* occurs at the beginning when Gil Blas robs his uncle in order to leave home and is immediately robbed and tricked himself. But this sequence is unique in the novel. The assault by reality on the picaro is quickly dissolved by Le Sage in the interest of his satire. Were it allowed to be important, it would shatter the tone of the whole book.

Moll Flanders, on the other hand, prominently features the fast rhythm pattern, but it differs from most picaresque novels in that the fast rhythm generally occurs only toward the end. Though there is little of the fast rhythm pattern in that half of the book treating Moll's marriages, the latter half of the book exhibits trick following trick at a rapid rate. In the brief space of nine pages, for example, we find Moll performing five separate robberies (pp. 196-204). This rapid series of thefts has strategic importance in the structure of the novel, since it opens Moll's career as a thief and gives us the sense of instability in events that is to endure through one robbery after another until the end. While the rhythm is not quite so fast after the sequence just cited, it is still rapid. The effect is not merely the bewildering one of incident following incident, however. In each of the episodes almost breathlessly presented to us, the reader feels the continual danger Moll is in. Every separate robbery makes us hold our breath for her safety. The total effect of the rapid series of all the crimes is not only to bombard our sensibilities with incident, but also to wrack our nerves with anxiety.

The effect of the rapid event pattern in *Roderick Random* is a bit different and more typical of our group of novels. Unlike most of the bombardment in *Moll Flanders,* here the rush of events is accompanied by violence, ugliness, and pain. As in *Guzmán, Simpli-*

cissimus, and *El Buscón,* these picaresque motifs contribute to the protagonist's loss of sanity. In Chapter 24 Roderick, lately recovered from venereal disease, is accosted by a press gang. He defends himself, laying one man "motionless on the ground," but is captured after receiving a "large wound on my head, and another on my left cheek." Taken to a "pressing tender" and put in the hold, he experiences the reaction of madness to the mad picaresque world: "I was thrust down into the hold among a parcel of miserable wretches, the sight of whom well-nigh distracted me." Not having his wounds bandaged, and not being able to bandage them himself, he gives his handkerchief to a fellow prisoner, asking him to tie up his bleeding head. The fellow takes the handkerchief and promptly sells it to a bum-boat woman "for a quart of gin." When the miserable Roderick complains of the robbery and his bleeding wounds to the midshipman on deck, that officer squirts "a mouthful of dissolved tobacco upon . . . [him] through the gratings." He adds insult to injury telling Roderick that he "was a mutinous dog and that . . . [he] might die and be d----d" (2, 31-32).

All these events are recounted in the space of one page. The rush of events is coupled with Roderick's going mad and all the shock effect of violence and pain. The *moral* order we expect (or hope to find) in life has also dissolved. In this rush of event we find an image of the world's deep disorder, typical of nearly all the novels we are considering. I do not think it too much to say that the reader is shocked by the relatively unusual literary subject matter [27] into a state resembling that of the swooning hero. We may tentatively define this sympathetic swooning, this reeling of the reader's senses, as the affective sum of the devices in the picaresque novel.

IV

Fortune

HE EPISODIC PLOT, TO-
gether with the rapid rhythm of events, combines with the Fortune
pattern to give the picaresque plot its characteristic form and effect.
The dizzying alternations in the hero's fortunes emphasize the
chaotic structure of reality. The picaresque hero is continually assaulted by events, but unlike other fictional heroes, he can ultimately
do little to control these events. His fortune goes up or down as it
pleases. His fate is in the lap of the gods, but the gods are continually dropping it. Haphazard revolutions of good and bad fortune
are his lot, and in the senseless and unstoppable whirling, we may be
made to feel the instability of our own fortunes.

In the picaresque novel the classical and Renaissance motif of
Fortune dominates the entire action. Moreover, the whole pica-
resque tradition is full of statements, laments, and complaints about
Fortune. Jack Wilton, for example, says:

> So it fortuned (fie upon that unfortunate word of fortune) that
> this whore, this quean, this courtezan, this common of ten
> thousand, so bribing me not to bewray her, had given me a
> great deal of counterfeit gold, which she had received of a coiner
> to make away a little before [p. 246].

Fortune and luck call the turn elsewhere in *The Unfortunate Traveller* (e.g., pp. 286, 290), but only *Guzmán de Alfarache,* among the
early picaresque novels, has a narrative sizable enough to demon-

28

strate the theme of Fortune in its plot pattern and to develop it fully by suitable reflections.

In the fourth volume of Mabbe's translation we find two long revolutions of Guzmán's career punctuated by apostrophes to Fortune. At the end of the Second Book, Second Part, Chapter ix, Guzmán celebrates the culmination of a long period of success won by his cunning and his good luck. He has more than recovered the value of his stolen clothes, he has revenged himself on his relatives in Genoa, and apparently he has escaped scot-free in a galley. He is preparing to return to his homeland and even gets to see "the coast of Spaine" without mishap. It is at this propitious point, however, that Guzmán's wheel takes a mad whirl and we are off again. He announces the coming disasters thus: "But fortune, having not the strength to stand firme, nor being alwayes one and the same; but weake and various, began to manifest unto us the small confidence that we ought to have of her" (*4*, 35).[28] When they are within sight of Spain, a storm blows up; much of Guzmán's property is ruined; and his friend Sayavedra gets sick, goes mad, and kills himself by jumping into the sea.

The sea storm, of course, is an old and useful symbol for man's helplessness before the revolution of outer circumstance, but the sudden revolutions of Guzmán's fortune are not restricted to the sea. What we have just seen is a short fall after the long rise following an earlier fall in Rome. But Guzmán's life is never really secure. When he has established himself as a merchant in Madrid and all seems to be going well, he announces the coming fall again by reference to Fortune: "There did I live, with that poore trading that I had, like a *Fucar;* and there should I have ended my dayes like a Prince, if my hard fortune, and greedy ill lucke had not crost me, by the unhappy encounter of a crafty knave, with a covetous wretch" (*4*, 126).[29] Then Guzmán marries the wrong woman and ends in bankruptcy.

Since Guzmán did not *have* to get married and so lose his success and stability, we must admit that part of his fall is his own fault. Even so, the temptations which are thrown in our way and his are not ordered by us or him. The numbers that come up for us are not of our choosing. It is the unique resource of the picaresque novel to vividly explore and lament the hopeless whirl of Fortune in which we are all involved.

In comedy—the comic tales in Boccaccio's *Decameron* are an example—the central image of life is man pitted against Fortune.

The astute bend it to their will; the dull fall to Fortune, and to the astute. In the picaresque novel, all are caught in a whirl of events that constantly works on their weaknesses whenever they have asserted their strength, that senselessly raises them up only to strike them down. In comedy and the romance, the hero is usually able to reconcile himself with Fortune in a stable marriage. Fortune is shown conquered at last. But in the true picaresque novel there is no escape. Guzmán continually seeks some security from the ravages of Fortune: "I stood looking for a day, to set up my rest, and how to order the remaynder of my life in some settled course . . ." (*4*, 153). But all his efforts go for naught.

Guzmán had realized earlier that man cannot escape what life may decide to do with him:

> I will conclude this Chapter with telling thee; That when misfortune shall follow a man, no diligence, nor good counsell shall availe him; but shall, where hee thinks to gather wooll, goe away with his fleece shorne [*3*, 228].[30]

The theme of man's passivity before life's chaotic events is probably more important in the picaresque novel than the theme of *picardía* itself.

> Man proposeth one thing, and God disposeth another. Who would ever have dream't, that things would have fallen out as they doe? What should one say unto it? There is now no helpe for it. For as a man cannot avoyde the stone, which a foole throwes by chance over a house, and kills him therewith: So, much lesse was it to be imagined . . . that such a businesse . . . should prove so disproportionable, and so quite opposite to our understanding [*3*, 242].[31]

The stone image here seems to express perfectly the sense of life revealed in most of the novels we are considering. If the realistic novel, broadly speaking, expresses the probable and predictable universe of science and social science, the picaresque novel seems to express an unpredictable universe where Fortune holds sway. If God is mentioned in the first line here, it is only to say He is irrational as far as man can understand Him.

Though shorter in length and narrower in scope of action than *Guzmán de Alfarache, El Buscón* exhibits the same Fortune pattern. Pablos' fortune rises and falls. The son of a barber and a witch, he comes within a hair's breadth of marrying a rich aristocrat, but ends with his face slashed and his pockets empty. He gets a legacy from his parents, but ends by wasting it in prison and by preparing the impotent plot for the marriage just mentioned. Previously, he has come close to seducing his landlord's daughter, but falls (literally falls, from a roof while trying to get to the girl's bedroom) and is beaten. He accumulates some money in Alcalá, but is cheated out of it by a card-sharp "hermit." In the next to last paragraph of the novel, Pablos is forced, like other picaresque heroes, to realize that Fortune runs life, at least his life: "Fortune was unrelenting in her castigations of me . . ." (p. 233).[32] As in other picaresque novels, Fortune is seen here as persecuting the hero because he is immoral. One may argue, however, as others have done, that this moralizing of Fortune is merely put on for the Inquisition. Similar statements also occur in *Guzmán,* but the central vision, in both novels, remains not one of God's punishing a sinner but of life's chaotic structure, of arbitrary Fortune's punishing a man who is no better or worse than most men. After all, most picaresques identify the picaro with all other men.[33]

If we turn now to our next major example, *Simplicissimus* (1669), we must conclude that the Fortune pattern has become fixed as a prominent aspect of the picaresque novel. Indeed, in his staggeringly episodic plot Grimmelshausen has managed more revolutions of Fortune per page than perhaps any other picaresque writer. Consequently, the book is full of statements about the uncertainty of human prosperity and stability, which transform the background of the Thirty Years War into a metaphor for picaresque uncertainty.[34] Simplicissimus' fortunes rise and fall, but even in periods of prosperity Grimmelshausen is careful to warn us of the coming fall. The reader's exhilaration at the picaro's victory over chaotic experience is carefully and continually dampened by such statements as these: ". . . the well-known fortune-teller in that town [Soest] advised me, and told me likewise I had more enemies in Soest and in mine own regiment than outside the town and in the enemy's garrisons: and these, said she, were all plotting against me and my money" (p. 107).[35] Simplicissimus also cautions himself in his prosperity: "I reflected at times that nothing is so certain in this world as its uncertainty. And so I must fear if ever Fortune should let loose her hornets upon me it would altogether overwhelm my present happiness" (p. 183).[36] Sometimes he ascribes his coming fall to his own character (in reality, his fall is due to other circumstances: the bankruptcy of the merchant who has his savings in Cologne and the knavery of the innkeeper who sends him to France): "But with my good fortune my pride so increased that in the end it could bring me nothing but a fall" (p. 185).[37]

Such dark predictions help to differentiate this novel and others we are examining from pure comedy. When Laurel and Hardy, or the Marx brothers, pull off the most incredible manipulations of a situation, the audience rejoices in the comic hero's mastery of the world. But the picaro never attains this kind of comic mastery for long, and therefore the audience reading his story is never exalted by its identification with him. Even in the revels of success, the sobering threat of fall exists.

And that there is no escape from chaos, no matter how astute the manipulator of events, is proved by the disasters that pursue Simplicissimus. When, to take a single example, he is given a magic stone by the spirits of the Mummelsee with which he can produce a mineral spring on earth, his hopes for a prosperous spa are dashed when the stone falls from his pocket in a forest far from home. There is no stability, no enduring success or security for Simplicissimus or for most picaresque heroes. Where Fortune and Chance rule the world, neither is there any lasting comic joy.[38]

In *Gil Blas,* however, the Fortune pattern has been altered. This alteration further contributes to the change in tone and effect that we have already found in *Gil Blas.* It is of course true that the Fortune pattern appears in the novel. For one thing, it is loaded with references to Fortune.[39] One would gather from such references that Gil Blas experiences a tremendous number of ups and downs, and, to be sure, his fortune does vary. He no sooner gets a master than he loses him. He is elevated to the confidence of the Prime Minister, the Duke of Lerma, and then cast into prison. He receives a diamond ring, is swindled out of it, recovers it, and then loses it again to jailers.

Yet despite such ups and downs, and despite all the references to Fortune in the novel, the Fortune pattern is very much muted here. For one thing, the edge is taken off Fortune's effect on the character. True, Gil Blas is thrust into prison and robbed of his ring (I, 2, v), but within three days he is released and returns to lucrative service with Doctor Sangrado. True, he is driven from this illustrious master (in the same chapter) by a Biscayan *miles gloriosus* enraged at the death of his intended bride under Gil Blas's medical care. But no sooner is he out of this job than he meets Diego de la Fuente on the road (I, 2, vi, 145), is befriended, and is recommended to Matheo Melendez in Madrid, who gets him another job. Gil Blas loses masters apace, but he is never plunged very far into the depths by

32

Fortune. Even Gil Blas's most dramatic fall, from Prime Minister's confidant to political prisoner, is a gentle one (III, 9, iv, 95). He is always more or less secure. Leading an almost enchanted existence, he makes his way comfortably from master to master.

Moreover, Gil Blas is a picaro surrounded by supporters—notably Don Alphonso's family. In fact, Don Caesar promises Gil Blas, after the latter's fall under the Duke of Lerma, "You should no longer be the sport of Fortune. I will deliver you from her power, by securing to you a property which she cannot take from you" (III, 9, x, 140).[40] And Don Caesar is as good as his word. In the last two books of the novel (there are twelve), Gil Blas's fortune never descends below that of a landed gentleman.

Gil Blas himself sums up well his relatively good treatment by Fortune. He reflects that he should not have despaired after having been deserted by Count Galiano: "After so often experiencing that Fortune had no sooner cast me down than she raised me up again, I ought merely to have regarded my sad condition as a harbinger of speedy prosperity" (II, 7, xvi, 342).[41] The book thus breeds an easy optimism, a sense of security in the face of Fortune, totally new in the main picaresque tradition. If Fortune has not been killed here, she has at least been tamed. With this taming, the emotional effects, if not the picture, of a chaotic world disappear.

One would think the muting of the change of Fortune pattern in *Gil Blas* might be found in *Moll Flanders*. But despite all the moralizing in *Moll Flanders,* despite the apparent security of the heroine at the end, despite the suggestion of a religious Providence that rewards the penitent and punishes the sinner, we must admit that the major plot pattern of *Moll Flanders* is one of Fortune. The word "Fortune" is only mentioned occasionally in the novel (e.g., p. 271), but the pattern of Fortune is everywhere stamped on the book's action. Moll experiences a great number of highs and lows, and her search for security never seems satisfied until the end.[42] Because of her attractive appearance and pleasant manner, she is raised from early poverty to a position of security in a middle-class household. Having all her young life longed for security, she accepts the prospect of an "easy, prosperous life" (p. 52) in marriage, though the man she marries happens to be the brother of the man she loves. Her position as a poor single woman is desperate and therefore her search for security is equally desperate. Yet the security she finds in her first marriage is short lived, for her husband dies at "the end of five years" (p. 54). With this blow to her stable position begins the assault of Fortune which is to destroy every perch she may find and which is to dominate the first half of the novel.

The reader is dazed as husband after husband comes and goes, each unstable marriage leaving Moll older and less secure than in the previous one. The first husband dies after five years, but the second, who seems both a gentleman and a tradesman, lasts only two and one-quarter years, after which time he goes bankrupt and flees to France. To secure her diminishing fortunes, Moll marries again, passing herself off as a rich widow. But the Virginia planter she marries eventually turns out to be her own brother! "What miserable chance could bring thee hither?" exclaims her mother in Virginia (p. 93). On returning to England she is not even fortunate enough to secure a husband at first. Instead she lives for six years with a gentlemen who in the end deserts her, leaving her a paltry fifty pounds. As she gets older and poorer and less good looking, the search for security becomes more desperate still: "I wanted to be placed in a settled state of living," she often exclaims (e.g., p. 128), but the settled state she expects to find with each new husband eludes her as it has with his predecessors. The apparently rich Irishman she thinks she has landed turns out to be more a pauper than she is. This marriage lasts merely a few weeks. Naturally, the duration of security seems even shorter to the reader than to Moll, since it is usually summed up in a short phrase (e.g., "two years and a quarter he broke," p. 58). We see, that is, Moll's continual elevation and fall, only "hearing" about her period of security in some brief summary.

This inexorable movement of Fortune continues unabated until Moll is too old to gain security by marriage and is forced to rob. Though she is a successful thief for a long while, in the end she falls again. Moreover, the sense of instability generated by the Fortune pattern in the marriage part is maintained in the thievery part by the continual threat of apprehension and execution by the law.

Smollett, like Defoe, did not follow Le Sage's muting of the Fortune pattern. Though he admitted modeling *Roderick Random* on the "method" and "plan" of *Gil Blas,* he emphasized that the Fortune pattern and especially the misfortunes of the hero were to be stressed more than in *Gil Blas*. This stress is intended to be morally shocking, exciting "that generous indignation which ought to animate the reader against the sordid and vicious disposition of the world" ("The Preface," *1,* xli). Looking at the novel from the perspective of the whole genre, we can see the Fortune pattern in *Roderick Random* as creating not only a picture of the moral vices of mankind, but also a picture of the instability of the world in an almost metaphysical sense. It is an instability which seems to be part of the nature of the novel's world. That Roderick's falls in fortune are painful, more painful perhaps than those of our other protagonists, only serves to emphasize the disorder in reality. Moreover, not all of Roderick's falls in fortune are man's doing. The shipwreck on the English coast and Roderick's loss of money at the gaming tables of Bath are both examples of the gyrations of Fortune's wheel not dependent on man's sordid disposition. Finally, if that disposition is really part of mankind, then it is itself a propensity built into the race to wreak chaos in the world. Up to the romantic ending, the world of *Roderick Random* seems as uncontrollable as the worlds of most of our classic picaresque novels.

V

Accident

N A SENSE, EVERY event in the picaresque is an accident since the episodic plot does not emphasize causality. Yet certain lightning-strikes of reality can be isolated as a separate device in the picaresque plot. We find such a pure accident early in *El Buscón*. Pablos has been elected King of the Roosters in a Shrovetide student procession (p. 91). As he rides along, his horse bends down and eats a vegetable from a market stall. This accident immediately leads to a riot, with the vegetable sellers attacking the students. Pablos, who has been expecting a day of triumph, ends by falling off his horse into a latrine.[43]

This first accident is only one of several. The incident of Pablos' falling off the roof where he has climbed to court a lady has been mentioned in another connection. Naturally, punishment is swift and greater than might first seem likely. In its violence, it differentiates the picaresque from mere comedy. Pablos is thoroughly beaten by a notary and his men. They seize him for a thief, and he barely escapes being thrown into jail by bribing his way out of the tangle. A similar incident occurs when Pablos is innocently paying his rent to his landlady (who happens to be a bawd), and the place is raided:

> At the precise moment the officers entered my chamber, Maude and I were sitting on the bed together. The police closed in on us and with several lusty thwacks, threw me to the floor . . . her lover (a fruiterer who was in an inner room) made his escape. When the police saw him and found out from one of the guests

that I was not the real culprit, they bolted out after the scoundrel and seized him, leaving me all bruised and battered [p. 215].[44]

Why is the picaro so randomly punished by the world? In comedy, such punishment would come to the comic antihero: the *alazon,* the miser, the *miles gloriosus.* There, the punishment would be deserved. It would assert some universal order. But why does it happen here? There is no answer, just as there is no order in Pablos' world. Anything can happen to anyone at any time.

In *Gil Blas,* two accidents that typify the progress of the picaresque plot happen to Diego the barber. As Diego is going to an evening assignation at a married woman's house, the picaresque world dumps its excrement upon him:

> I went groping along the street, and had perhaps gone half the way, when from a window I was crowned with the contents of a vessel which did not exactly tickle my olfactory nerves. I may safely say that I lost none of it, so well was it directed [I, 2, vii, 161-62]! [45]

Another accident happens to Diego on a subsequent night. When his lady fair does not come to the door, he begins to signal to her by imitating a cat's meow. When the lady fails to appear he persists:

> I acquitted myself so well that a neighbor, who was coming home, taking me for one of the animals whose cries I was imitating, picked up a stone lying at his feet, and threw it at me with all his might, saying "Curse the cat!" I received the blow on my head, and was so stunned for the moment that I had well nigh fallen. I felt that I was badly hurt. Nothing more was needed to disgust me with gallantry . . . [I, 2, vii, 173].[46]

This may appear to be merely an example of comic punishment for an immoral, antisocial act, but it is not. The typical picaro of our novels is consistently assaulted by reality in a more violent, disgusting, and disordered way than perhaps any other literary hero. Yet we should note that in these two examples it is Diego who is assaulted and not Gil Blas—a minor character in his own framed story, not the hero of the novel. If such accidents happened to Gil Blas, the special muting of tone which we have found in this novel could not occur.

The accident pattern is used centrally, however, and with special effect in *Moll Flanders.* Moll attempts to steal a woman's watch and fails. Alarmed that the watch didn't come away when she pulled, quick-thinking Moll "let it go that moment and cried as if I had been killed, that somebody had trod upon my foot and that there was certainly pickpockets there, for someone or other had given a pull at my watch" (p. 217). The woman with the watch cries out too, and the crowd takes it up: "At that very instant, a little farther in the crowd, and very luckily too, they cried out 'A pickpocket' again, and really seized a young fellow in the very fact" (p. 217). Such an incredible accident as this enforces the sense of confusion that the disjointed episodic plot and Fortune pattern develop. Pure chance rules here, and the improbable is as likely to happen as the "probable" of the realistic novel. A further effect of such an incident is to enhance the sense we get from *Moll Flanders* that the supposed stability of the middle-class world is constantly threatened by an underworld that is everywhere intermixed with it. Within any crowd, the incident implies, if you shout "pickpocket" you are as likely as not to find one. It almost begins to seem as if there are more criminals than honest people—the picaresque world is not only morally identifiable with the corrupt middle-class world of *Moll Flanders* but also engulfs the middle-class world in the novel's action.[47]

The accident pattern we have been describing is not predominant in the picaresque, though many more examples might be cited. Instead, the recording of an occasional event of pure chance seems to focus the whole picaresque chaos. Accident seems to serve the function of recalling the chaotic world even when Roderick Random is escaping from it in the romantic ending of his story. Having found his newly rich father, Roderick, on the way back to his home and his bride like a good comic or romance hero, stumbles across a pair of picaresque accidents that seem strangely out of place in this conventional happy ending. He records, in passing, that "a sailor, having drank more new rum that he could carry, staggered overboard, and, notwithstanding all the means that could be used to preserve him, went to the bottom and disappeared" (*3*, 194). Also by accident, Roderick's ship happens to encounter another man floating in the sea: "he had fallen overboard about four-and-twenty hours ago, and the ship being under sail, they did not choose to bring to, but tossed a hencoop overboard for his convenience . . ." (*3*, 195). These incidents, so out of place in the merry tone of rejoicing that dominates the ending, seem to be Smollett's denial (conscious or unconscious) of the *truth* of that comic-romance ending. Inserted into

Roderick's new stable world, they deny it by recalling the metaphysical anarchy that has bitterly dominated the book.

These accidents in the picaresque make the reader uneasy. The normal man, at least in the prosperous West today, lives by the assumption that everything will be ordered and on time. But the reality that he finds in the picaresque corresponds in external action to the sense of internal and external chaos many feel threatening their superficially ordered lives. We know that sometimes life is not smooth, and that often our inner lives, our moods and random feelings, are anything but controlled and ordered. To a considerable extent, the morning newspaper is made up of accounts of disorder in the world—a race riot, a war, a rape, a bizarre and seemingly comic accident, a theft, an embezzlement, a protest and an angry reply. The picaresque novel increases our perceptions and expectations of such tumult. We come to expect after reading of picaresque accidents that if we step out of the house, a safe, a chamber pot, or a stone surely and inexplicably will strike us down. The train that takes us to the office will surely be late because somebody will have derailed it or jumped in front of it. And the office will have burned down by the time we get there. The accident pattern, though it does not pervade the picaresque novel, contributes markedly to the sense of chaos.

Part Two

Character

". . . the inconstant Figure of this insuing discourse."
—Alfonso de Baros

I

The Picaro and Real Characters; The Picaro and Other Literary Characters; Plan of Part Two

OST PEOPLE SEARCH
for stability and security. This search takes both outward and inward forms. Outwardly, it is for such things as a steady job, public reputation, a house with paid-up mortage, a secure family relationship, and so forth. They seek to anchor their fluctuating inner lives in such things as a steady emotion (love), a meaningful vocation, a moral code, a religious or philosophic answer. Naturally, internal and external stability are closely related in any given human being, but for purposes of analysis we may separate the inner from the outer man, the inner quest from the outer one.

In examining the examples of inner stability, it will be seen that the search is for a *definition* of personality, for a unity, for what has been called *integrity*. It may be fair to say that most people, much of their lives, are very far from attaining this sense of wholeness and stability. The hero of each novel under consideration here is a disordered literary character, and in his external and internal instability one may find a reflection, albeit an exaggerated one, of the inner chaos that so many people feel. Herein is the meaning of what we may call the form, or structure, of the picaro's character.

While our typical protagonist expresses only disorder in his random character structure, many other literary heroes express in their calculated structures some sense of internal order. The picaro differs in this way from the comic hero, the romance hero, and the tragic hero.

Comic personages may be divided into two principal types, the butts and the wits.[1] The butt is conventionally defined, by comedy and its critics, as a flat comic character. Each butt has one trait, each embodies one type, e.g., the miser, the cuckold. And, as Maynard Mack has said, the butt's all-sufficient destiny is to go on exposing himself in his singleness of personality.[2] Clearly, no sense of instability is generated by such a flat comic character. On the contrary, he seems *too* stable, and opposite him stands his rounder enemy, the wit.

The wit is usually a poised character in control of a situation of which the butt is the butt. But for the purposes of comedy, this character is also tightly ordered. For example, though Ser Ciappelletto, in Boccaccio's first tale in the *Decameron,* dodges and weaves in and out to take advantage of others, he emerges as well defined as the butts he takes advantage of. They are defined by their single trait of stupid credulity; he is defined by his single trait of pure intelligence. He is interested *solely* in duping the credulous and thereby asserting his own ego. In more complicated comedies, the butts and wits are often the same persons, who discard their buttish parts to join together in marriage as defined "normal personalities." Elizabeth loses her prejudice; Darcy, his pride. Even Célimène, at the end of *The Misanthrope,* may be about to lose her vanity; Alceste, his misanthropy and his bad temper. But going into such considerations would take us far afield. Suffice it to say here that the comic hero, flat or round, butt or wit, eccentric or normal, usually has a rigorously and narrowly *defined* personality.[3]

Such personality structures, in their very definiteness, transmit a sense of order and joy. We rejoice at the order of the butt because it is comprehensible, although manifestly inadequate. We rejoice at the more sophisticated order of the wit because it is comprehensible and more than adequate. Identifying ourselves with the wit, we exult in his single-minded, non-problematic solution to life's circumstances and in his victory over the transparent butt. When Ser Ciappelletto triumphs because he is amorally interested in *only* that, we rejoice in the victory of intelligence. He imposes his ordered personality on the world and makes it stick. He succeeds because he attains a greater definition of personality than most of us ever do.

Like the comic hero, the romance hero is also defined and ordered. Instead, however, of having only *one* trait or interest, he embodies the singleness or unity of *perfection* in an accumulation of good qualities. Ozmin and Daraxa are useful examples.[4] She is all beautiful, all virtuous, and even speaks perfect Spanish. He is handsome, courageous, intelligent, virtuous, and resourceful. All of these qualities are constants which do not waver; all of them line up symmetrically, showing a perfect ordering of perfect qualities. Here, as in many romances, the characters are also internally ordered by a single, overriding emotion that brings all their perfections into special focus—love. The love they feel for each other is as perfect as they are. To such characters, our response is again joy at their order. They are the ultimately stable beings of literature whom nothing can sway, nothing change. Some romance heroes have no love interest but have an ideal (Parsifal and the Grail), or have merely a sense of heroic vocation (Beowulf), but in any case, the character's structure is defined and the reader's response is joy in the ordered definition.

The tragic hero is more complicated. He, if we may oversimplify again, starts as partially defined and reaches definition only at the end, and often at the cost, of his life. Such is the course, for example, of both Antony and Cleopatra in Shakespeare's play. As Thomas McFarland has shown,[5] both these characters are disordered at the beginning of the play by an internal tension between their interest in love and their interest in the world. Struggling with this disordering tension throughout the drama, wracked by it, they only reach final definition at the end when each gives up his life and the world in order to define his personality by love. The tragic hero at last sees things clearly and defines himself and his destiny in some final act. The stability we labor for all our lives he finds in two hours on the stage, and our joy in this swift ordering is proportionate to the compression of the process.

The hero of picaresque novels is typically opposed to these characters in whose inner stability, whether throughout the work (comic, romance) or at the end (tragic), we feel joy and exaltation. To put it another way: the picaro is neither a round nor a flat character. A flat character is defined by one trait; a round character, by the organic interrelation or organization of his traits.[6] The picaro differs from the flat in having many traits, from the round in having shifting traits that present no order, that seem random in their appearances and disappearances and connections. While most literary characters speak for the ordered side of our personalities, he speaks for the disordered side.

All these observations will lack meaning unless they are explored in a thorough description of our typical hero's character. Rather than merely cataloguing trait after trait, it seems best to approach the picaro from several points of view, considering at different times his origins, certain of his traits, his personal organization of traits, his relation to the outer world, and so forth. Only through such a complex approach can we come close to the total *figura* of the picaro and to its total significance.

II

Origins

HE ORIGINS OF THE
picaresque hero are both an anticipatory symbol and a social cause of
his inner chaos.[7] When Alfonso de Baros, Chamberlain to Philip
III, wrote a prefatory "Elogio" of Mateo Alemán's *Guzmán de
Alfarache,* he referred to Guzmán as "the inconstant Figure of this
insuing discourse" (Mabbe, *1*, 22).[8] Though he and the author
looked upon the novel as urging people to a contrary steadiness of
character, this steadiness was only to have been *exhibited* in the
Third Part, and the Third Part was never written. This fact suggests
that for all Alemán's moral intent, for all his feeling that steadiness
of character was essential in life, he could not find very much
steadiness to represent either in people or in the structure of the
world.

In any event, even the account of Guzmán's birth prepares us for
an "inconstant Figure" embodying an anarchy found everywhere in
the novel. In the first place, Guzmán is not even really certain who
his father is. His mother makes both the old knight (to whom she
is married) and another man each believe that he is Guzmán's
father: "Both of them did acknowledge me to be their sonne; the
one sayd, I was his; so did the other" (*1*, 84).[9] Up to this point
Guzmán speaks as though he knows that the second man and not
the knight was his father. He even records that he resembles the
merchant. But actually, we learn, all that Guzmán knows about his
birth his mother told him, and she has already been characterized as
a liar. The reader gradually becomes aware that Guzmán's origins

are a matter of mere conjecture. In the end, Guzmán is forced to admit he does not really know who his father is, but *decides* to accept the merchant who claimed him as a son after his mother's knight-husband died: "I call my selfe his sonne, and so I take my selfe to be: since that from that Mellon-bed I was made legitimate by the holy right of Matrimony. And it is much better for me this way, then that people should say, that I am ill-borne, and the sonne of no man" (*1*, 85).[10]

But if the chaos of Guzmán's character is built into him, metaphorically, by his uncertain origins, it is raised to the second power by the equally uncertain origins of his parents. *If* the merchant is his father, then we must discover who the merchant is, but his identity is shrouded from us too: "But be it as it may be, and grant that this Easterling, this Jew, or this Moore be my father . . ." (*1*, 85).[11] Guzmán's father has gone through four religions, having been first a Jew, then a Christian, then a Moslem, and finally a Christian again. What is he really, we ask. He is nothing more than a chaos of appearances, as ill defined as the picaro who appears to be his son.

Guzmán's mother is not much different in this regard. Her origins are even more in doubt than the picaro's because her own mother played the same game she did, passing off her daughter on a number of different men. Guzmán first tells us: "If my Mother brought two into the net, my Grandmother brought two doozen . . ." (*1*, 89).[12] But in the next paragraph, the number is fantastically increased: "With this daughter of hers, (I meane my Mother) she insnared a hundred severall persons, vowing and protesting to every supposed father, that my Mother was his child, and so to all, that she was like them all: To such a one, in her eye; to another, in her mouth . . ." (*1*, 89).[13] Guzmán's mother herself doesn't know who *her* real father was and chooses the surname of Guzmán because her mother liked it: "in discharge whereof, she [Guzmán's mother] did verily beleeve, and was fully perswaded (by some likely incounters, probably ghesses, and other circumstances of time and place jumping and concurring together) that she was some by-blow of a Cavallero, that was neere of kinne to the Dukes of Medina Sidonia" (*1*, 90).[14]

Thus does Guzmán first come on stage, a character involved in a mangle of guesses and suppositions. The incredible confusion surrounding his origins stands as a metaphor for his future character. Surely, the reader feels, no stable character can come out of such eccentric origins: we are to meet a type of literary character different from any other, in the same way his origins are different from those of other literary characters.[15]

In addition to its functions as metaphor for the picaro's character, the chaos of origins has a function in the action. The unstable family situation of the picaro sends him away from home on his picaresque journey. Guzmán indicates this when he summarizes his reasons for going out into the world: "I was an unfortunate man . . . and stood alone by my selfe, without any tree by me, either to shadow or to shelter me" (*1*, 92).[16]

It is even possible to understand this chaos of origins from another point of view—the psychology of character and reader. We have already referred to the reader's psychology in his possible identification with the picaro. But the reader knows, without psychologists telling him, that a person's ignorance about who or what his parents are is a circumstance calculated to create a feeling of insecurity in that person. When we are confronted with a fictional character whose origins are confused, we are prepared, if we know anything about how real people grow up, for a character who will reflect those origins.

The Buscón's origins are like Guzmán's. He doesn't really know his mother's background, and the identity of his father is a mystery since his mother is a whore. When he confronts her with the public rumor that he may not be the son of the man he thinks is his father, his mother replies with an evasion: "You understand all about such things, don't you? . . . You are a very clever lad . . . [but] even if such things are true, they had better be left unsaid" (pp. 89-90).[17] Born like Guzmán into a world of ambiguous appearances, Pablos is told to hide his real identity under a mask or not to try to search it out. Shocked at not knowing who his parents are, he determines to leave home in search of stability as a would-be gentleman. But he will never find the stability, either inner or outer, that he seeks.

Simplicissimus learns who his parents are, but only at the end. What is more significant about his origin, however, is that his mother gives birth in the midst of the Thirty Years War, the novel's dominating symbol of life's chaos. This is clearly a variation of the usual picaresque birth into the chaos of the underworld. I have saved until now any mention of the picaro's underworld origins; first, in order to stress other aspects of those origins; and, second, because the underworld pattern has often been too narrowly interpreted. Much has been written about the sociology of the picaro's origins from a historical point of view. Del Monte, for example, who has written one of the most sensitive discussions of the picaresque novel, spends much time tracing the appearance of a picaresque class of vagabonds in Spain to the lack of a middle class.[18] The implication is that the picaresque novel owes its origins to Spanish history and is an imitation of a particular aspect of Spanish history. But the picaro's origins are of more than historical interest. The dark under-world into which Guzmán and Pablos are born does not differ in literary effect from the chaotic war into which Simplicissimus is born. Both war and underworld anticipate the dark overworld the character will discover, anticipate the darkness of the character-to-be, and help determine the character by assuring that he will encounter more of life's irregularity than most of us.

Having discovered in *Gil Blas* fundamental modifications of the usual picaresque plot and pattern, we are not surprised to note similar subtle modifications in the structure of the main character. These, like the earlier modifications, help take *Gil Blas* out of the central stream of picaresque fiction, although they secure for it a place of stature in comic fiction. Since this section on origins is our first discussion of character in the picaresque novel, it will be well to postpone consideration of the origins question in *Gil Blas* in order to consider first the general difference between its treatment of charac-ter and the treatment of character found in the other novels we are discussing. Then we can go on to trace particular modifications in characterization in *Gil Blas*.

In these novels, the picaro's experiences are important as a picture of the chaos of the world, but those experiences are always person-ally felt and mediated by him. When reading these novels, we perceive not merely a view of chaos in the outside world, but also a sense of how it *feels* to be in such a world and how that world makes a man internally disordered. In *Gil Blas,* there is little focus on the picaro himself. Therefore, in reading this book any observa-tions we may make about the protagonist's Protean or unstable qualities [19] are of minor importance since he himself is of minor importance in *Gil Blas*. We may find a hint here or there that makes Gil Blas seem like a true picaro, but because of his slight role in the novel these occasional bits of characterization do not constitute a significant part of the novel's form or, therefore, of its content.

Gil Blas is focused squarely outward on the world until the eighth of its twelve books, when the focus shifts at last to the central hero. First, the innumerable frame stories inserted in the novel move the focus away from the picaro. He neither figures in these frame stories nor tells them. Even his early career is brief and is interrupted by the digression of the robbers' stories in Book I, Chapter v. Second, when Gil Blas tells the story in his own person, the focus is still not on *him,* but on what he sees. His many masters are characterized in great detail (Sangrado, Sedillo, etc.), but his actions or reactions to them are not detailed. This pattern obtains through Book VII and into Book VIII. Le Sage's main purpose is satirical and therefore different from our other novels. As in *Le Diable boiteux,* Le Sage is using his character as a device through which to encounter and describe various types of people and their foibles (Sangrado, the pedantic and incompetent doctor, or the young decadent noblemen [*1,* 208 ff.], or actors, etc.). Le Sage is not painting his protagonist as a picaro deranged by chaotic life, because Le Sage did not feel life as a bitter and irredeemable chaos. He felt life to be a funny and often stupid spectacle which a wise man would accept without much ado. For Le Sage, the world has only a number of deranged *types* (which, of course, many of us approach to some extent—e.g., we are all sometimes vain, pedantic, dishonest, hypocritical); it does not derange men as a rule into internal chaos. Le Sage can submerge his protagonist because he need not derange him.[20]

One might object, however, that mere digressions and an outward focus do not necessarily mean *Gil Blas* fails to develop the protagonist as a central part of its form and meaning. After all, it might be argued, there are digressions in *Guzmán* too, but the protagonist's centrality is apparent throughout. Such an objection might be valid if there were not a difference, albeit a subtle one, between *Guzmán* and *Gil Blas* in this respect. Whenever we read *Guzmán* we are aware, even in the digressions and outer description, of the voice and personality of the narrating ex-picaro. The personal meaning to the speaker of all the didactic reflections or descriptions of manners is constantly brought home with shocking picaresque effect. Such is not the case in *Gil Blas.* Of course the narrator of *Guzmán,* as of *Gil Blas,* is not the young rogue; he is the person who once was a rogue. Still, when the older Guzmán speaks we are aware, even in a didactic digression, of his importance as a character in the whole book. Therefore, when the *action* returns to focus on Guzmán the young rogue, we are vitally involved in his character and in his picaresque reactions to events. In *Gil Blas,* there is no such personal glow over outer events or descriptions—the character (both old reflecting narrator and young active picaro) has almost disappeared from the scene and the reader's concern.

The fact that this disappearance is not total, however, makes the classification of *Gil Blas* as non-picaresque a bit less easy than we have so far indicated. From Book VII on, the action focuses by and large on the picaro himself, and the mere description of outer manners and foibles is in part abandoned. By Book VIII, this focus has intensified, and it remains rather strong. Thus, roughly a third of *Gil Blas* focuses on the hero. Furthermore, the earlier portions of the novel (Books I-VII) contain hints of character which we should examine.

Gil Blas differs from other picaresque heroes first in his origins. There is no ambiguity about them. Who his father and mother are is clearly set forth in the first paragraph. But it is not only on the score of paternity that we find no metaphor in the picaro's origins for a chaotic character-to-be. Unlike Lazarillo, Guzmán, and Pablos, Gil Blas is not born into the underworld of roguery and crime. His parents are poor but respectable; his father has been a soldier and, like his mother, is now a servant. One of his uncles, a clergyman, educates Gil. In addition to lacking ambiguity of origins and criminal background, Gil Blas differs even from Simplicissimus in that he is not born into a symbolic anarchic circumstance like the Thirty Years War and is not separated from his parents by such a circumstance. Gil Blas's origins contrast with those of a true picaro who appears in the novel with him. Don Raphael's origins are quite ambiguous: "I am the son of an actress of Madrid, famous for her elocution, and still more for her gallantries. Her name was Lucinda. As for my father, it would be rash to name any one" (2, 123).[21] Here we have the same doubt about origins that we find in other picaros. Raphael, like a true picaro, grows up in the semicriminal world (as Le Sage sees it in *Gil Blas*) of the theatre. He is not educated in his early years, but left to his own whims. Far from growing up in security until the age of seventeen and only then leaving it (as does Gil Blas), Don Raphael is buffeted about by his early experience when he is unjustly and brutally treated by a nobleman's tutor. There is, then, everything in Raphael's origins to symbolize and encourage chaos of personality. There is nothing in Gil Blas's. We can surmise at the outset, from the difference between Gil's origins and those of the other picaros, that his later character will be different also.

The different fates of Don Raphael and Gil Blas, stemming as they do from their different origins, suggest Le Sage's non-picaresque purpose in altering the picaresque novel's traditional form. Gil Blas, the good, largely stable, but somewhat light-headed hero, is rewarded at the end of the novel with good fortune. Don Raphael, the born and bred picaro who succumbs to his inner chaos, becoming and remaining a picaro, is burned by the Inquisition. Le Sage does not see life as chaos, but as moral order in which the good (although buffeted about) will or should win. The evil, on the other hand, will or should be punished. Le Sage has the satirist's and comedian's interest in suggesting by his plot and characterization the moral way things actually do, or should, or can work. He is not interested in exposing a metaphysical chaos at the heart of things, as are the other novelists we are treating, but rather in affirming a moral order.

Moll Flanders' origins, however, do fit into the earlier pattern. She discovers her mother's identity midway through the book, but her father's identity is never known. This chaos of parentage is underscored by her place of birth, for Moll is born in Newgate. To complete the pattern, her first memory is of wandering among a crew "of those people they call gypsies" (p. 3). But having followed the traditional pattern thus far, Defoe manages a brilliant variation. Instead of continuing her early life amid such a chaotic environment, Moll early falls into a stable situation. She becomes a parish ward and then a kind of semi-adopted daughter of a rich middle-class family. In such a stable environment, subject to no cataclysmic historical force (e.g., the Thirty Years War), we might expect Moll to grow up stable. But she does not. And this is Defoe's most brilliant stroke. For he shows that, through the apparent stability of middle-class respectable life, a chaos of conflicting passions winds like a snake. The internal chaos of the elder brother who seduces her is one passion. His sister's deranging jealousy is another. The mother's avaricious desire to enhance the family fortune and prevent her son's marrying a nobody is a third. The injustice of organized society that will not give a poor single woman a chance to lead a comfortable life (unless she exploits her feminine charms to get a rich husband) is yet a fourth element making for a chaotic tangle in Moll's early life.

By first setting Moll into a middle-class environment and then showing her still made chaotic by it later, Defoe profoundly enriched the technique of the picaresque novel for projecting its central truth: chaos is universal. We will see in earlier books a somewhat different approach.[22] The social-outcast picaro tries to leave his disordered early environment and enter "normal" middle- or upper-class social life. Then he is frustrated and deranged by finding "normal" life as disordered as his earlier life. In *Moll Flanders,* the process of showing chaos to be universal is completed much sooner than in earlier picaresque novels.

As a result, *Moll Flanders* achieves a peculiar new effect. On the one hand, it is one of the first examples of "realism" in Ian Watt's sense.[23] The middle-class family and house that are Moll's early environment have a new solidity and order. Nowhere in the earlier literature I know is there a house with such a felt solidity, with such a "real" upstairs, for example. And where else in earlier literature is there such a convincing picture of the orderly *pattern* of family life, including the *pattern* of its disruptions (as in family quarrels)?[24] But within this "realistic" and therefore ordered setting, first by showing how it gives *birth* to a picaro, Defoe has revealed an underlying chaos. The tension between realistic-novel devices and picaresque-novel devices gives the book its peculiar force and generalized meaning. Just as the novel combines picaresque and realistic novel devices, so it combines the world views implied by those devices. Most readers, I suppose, think of themselves as living in the orderly world of the realistic novel, but Defoe shows that chaos reigns amidst the supposed order.

Our last touchstone, *Roderick Random,* is in some ways more troublesome to analyze than any of the others. A careful examination of Roderick's character reveals that it is neither picaresque nor wholly non-picaresque. The confusion in characterization is symptomatic of a deeper confusion throughout the book. It is for its picaresque vision that *Roderick Random* is chiefly remembered, and therefore we include it among our examples. No one can forget the vision of universal anarchy projected by the first visit to London and the voyages with Captain Oakum and Crampley. But if some parts of the book seem to represent the world as chaotic, others, for example the happy ending, seem to show it as ultimately ordered in the manner of the romance. Still others seem to show it as a struggle between good and evil, with good viciously oppressed and then melodramatically triumphant.

As one might expect from what has been said, Roderick Random's origins are not simply chaotic in the traditional manner. He knows who his parents are and who their parents were; he is raised by his family; and he is a member of the upper classes—not the underworld. Roderick Random should have a stable career as a member of the British ruling class. In his origins he is exposed not to a chaotic world, but to a melodramatically evil one. True, he knows his parents, but his wicked grandfather so oppresses them that one dies and the other flees. As a result, Roderick Random is left all alone to endure the tyranny of the world; in this respect his origins are picaresque.

Smollett so changes the typical pattern of origins because he is interested in exposing "the sordid and vicious disposition of the world" and in animating "generous indignation" in the reader (*1,* xli). Smollett is interested not only in universal roguery, but also in melodrama. He seems to say not only that the world is bad and chaotic, but also that it should be and could be better. We are therefore given a character whose origins are clear but who is deprived of his birthright by the world which destroys his family. We watch him grow up in stable surroundings, but also see him systematically oppressed by his relatives. In treating his character's origins, then, Smollett departs somewhat from picaresque tradition. In doing so, he helps point the way toward a sentimentalization of the picaresque that caused the genre to disappear for more than a century and a half. However, he did not sentimentalize his own book so much that it lacks the bite of earlier picaresque novels.

III

The Picaresque Education

HE PATTERN OF A REL-
ative innocent developing into a picaro because the world he meets is
roguish is *the* pattern which begins our typical picaresque novel.
What del Monte has written concerning *Guzmán de Alfarache* is
true for other picaresque heroes: "The psychology of Guzmán is in
fact conditioned by the initial encounter with a hostile, cruel, and
fraudulent society, against which he reacts by adopting those same
vices which he condemns in it." [25] Lazarillo, for example, goes off
with the blind beggar expecting to find another father who will love
him. Instead, he is taught not only that there is no love in the world,
but also that there are only tricks. The picaro is educated by the
blind man into a blind world: "although he was blind, he illumi-
nated me, and in his own way gave me the only education I ever
had" (p. 30).[26]

The beginnings of picaresque novels point, then, to a disordered
world which the hero affirms by joining. By becoming a trickster,
the hero makes the only choice other than suicide that the world
offers him. If the world is tricky, peopled by tricksters, the picaro
must either give up his personality to join the trickery or else perish.
The picaro always joins. But, and this must he underscored, the
pattern of education into roguery by the world reflects on the world
more than on the picaro. It is the world that is picaresque; the picaro
only typifies that world in his dramatic change from innocent to
trickster. In affirming the world's outer chaos by becoming a picaro,
the hero gives up hope of personality and order. Having become a

manipulator of appearances, the picaresque character settles into the non-reality of becoming an appearance himself.

Guzmán de Alfarache's education is typical.[27] Driven forth from his mother's house by poverty and want of supporters, and resolving to seek his fortune, Guzmán's view of the world is entirely trusting: "I went abroad to see the World, travelling from place to place, re-commending my selfe to God, and well-disposed people, in whom I had put my trust" (*1*, 92).[28] The stages of hunger through which the typical picaro passes early in his career prepare the way for his infection by the world's roguery. The pressure of want drives the innocent picaro into inner chaos. Watching through the picaro's eye, the reader experiences that internal chaos. Guzmán lays down the precept:

> Where good feeding fayleth, there no good followeth; no evil which aboundeth not, no pleasure that indureth, nor content to comfort us. All fret and chafe, and know not why, nor wherefore . . . I knew not what to doe with my selfe . . . I found my selfe betwixt feares and hopes . . . My thoughts began as fast to waver, as my feet did to wander . . . [*1*, 94-95].[29]

At this point in his education, Guzmán falls asleep hungry and wakes up "without knowing for a while where I was; so that me thought I was still as it were in a dreame" (*1*, 96).[30] Reality having applied enough sheer physical pressure to substantially unsettle the character, the stage is set for his further corruption.

The first trick the world plays on Guzmán is that a hostess serves him bad food. She saw, Guzmán says, "that I was a novice in the world, and look't like a good honest simple Youth" (*1*, 98).[31] The simplicity, goodness, and integrity of the young picaro are opposed here to the world's immoral trickery. But Guzmán begins early to learn to dissemble. He assumes an appearance when the Carrier begins, apparently, to laugh at him (*1*, 107); he will not call the Carrier to account because he is weaker than the Carrier. From him Guzmán also learns that life consists of appearances. The Carrier seems, at first, the very soul of generosity, not merely offering to let Guzmán ride on a mule, but even paying his way at the inns in which they stay: "Now (me thought) I saw Heaven opened, and my honest Carrier appearing unto me in the shape of an Angell" (*1*, 109).[32] When, much later, Guzmán is asked by the Carrier to pay for all these services, this is his dazed reaction: "When I heard this, I was almost ready to hang my selfe, it was the bitterest draught, that ere went downe my throat" (*1*, 232).[33]

Guzmán differs from most picaresque novels in that the development of the protagonist into a rogue is gradual and occupies a large portion of the book. At the end of Mabbe's first volume Guzmán is not yet a true trickster, but still a mere sufferer from the world's trickery and chaos. Yet he is beginning already to bear the stamp of that chaos, as when he is "accused . . . for a Thiefe, by way as it were of Prophecie, presaging what I should bee hereafter" (*1*, 234).[34] A brief ten pages later, the process has gone forward apace. Guzmán has taken a job as a stable boy at an inn, and the innkeeper, a representative of the world and its ways, teaches him roguery: "There I learned to steepe Barley in warme water, to make it increase a third part, and to give false measure . . ." (*1*, 245).[35] Where before Guzmán had railed against innkeepers who had cheated him, now he cheats innocent youths like himself by padding the bills of "fresh-water-Souldiers, that were but Novices and yong Travellers" (*1*, 246).[36]

Guzmán does not become an out-and-out picaro, however, until he leaves the inn to be a porter in Madrid. Once again, it is the pressure of the world, unwilling to give a job to such an untrustworthy looking beggar, that forces him to roguery (see *1*, 251). Though this is the beginning of his picaresque career outside society, we have seen that underworld roguery is only an exaggeration of the way of the world, not a departure from it. In speaking of the frauds of doctors, Guzmán memorably fixes the universal roguery that his early career discovered:

> To treat of this, would aske a long discourse. All goes topsie-turvy; all Kim, Kam; all, is tricks and devices; all Riddles and unknowne Mysteries; you shall not finde man, with man; we all live in ambush, lying in wait one for another, as the Cat, for the Mouse, or the Spider for the Fly; who roming carelessely up and downe, suffers her selfe to be taken by a slender thread, whilest that venemous vermine, seazing on her head, holds her fast, never leaving her, till shee hath kill'd her with her poison [2, 19-20].[37]

Because the world is this way, Guzmán's picaresque education continues throughout his lifetime. He can never fully master the trickery of the world by his own trickery. The world is too picaresque for even an experienced rogue.

The picaresque education of Pablos, el Buscón, has already been touched on in the discussion of plot and pattern, but certain aspects of it deserve elaboration. It must be reemphasized that Pablos came out of his home largely ignorant of life's trickery, intending to be a good man, a gentleman. He should have known better. His supposed father had affirmed to Pablos the universality of thievery and deceit. Mocking his son's aspirations to be a gentleman, he solemnly remarked: "He who does not steal in this world cannot survive." [38] Pablos' personal experience soon tells him he should have listened to this hard-earned parental wisdom.

His whole experience at Cabra's boarding school is one of deception. Cabra is a deceiver and a self-deceiver. He conceals his stinginess under the guise of morality. Everything except the water-thin stew he serves to his pupils is "vice and gluttony" according to him. But he is not a cunning hypocrite ultimately, since he dies from self-starvation, apparently having tricked himself.

Pablos' next adventures are filled with more deliberate trickery. The last trick the strangers at an inn play is important since, foreshadowing Pablos' future course, it is gratuitous. The students and ruffians defecate on some stones and watch a man, who is persuaded the stones are candy, bite into them. The deception is perfect, dissolving the borders between the real and the apparent: "they made the poor man believe he was bewitched" (p. 109).[39] The way of the world is being revealed here: all men are rogues, deceivers with no true personalities, and the innocent, it is predicted, will soon conform: "The innkeeper said: 'The young gentlemen, with a few initiations like this, will certainly mature right quickly'" (p. 109).[40] The numerous tricks played on Pablos and Don Diego at Alcalá convince Pablos that he has been going about things the wrong way: "'In Rome, do as the Romans do,' says a wise proverb. Heeding its lesson, I resolved to be a knave among knaves, and even to outdo the rest of them if I could" (p. 117).[41]

The pattern of picaresque education is most affecting in *Simplicissimus,* since the hero's very name stresses his original innocence. Simplicissimus is not born in the lap of corruption like other picaros, but brought up on a farm in a condition of archetypal purity: "I knew nought of God or man, of Heaven or hell, of angel or devil, nor could discern between good and evil . . . I . . . lived like our first parents in Paradise . . ." (p. 3).[42] Furthermore, this innocence is forged into holiness and piety when Simplicissimus is forced to leave his home and to take up with a pious hermit who has forsaken the chaotic world of men for the pure and stable one of devotion to God. The hermit writes goodness on the boy's soul as on a "blank unwritten tablet" (p. 19). In one brief sentence Simplicissimus anticipates his own corruption, records the corruption of the world, and further says that whatever happened the world was always more corrupt than he ever became: "that pure simplicity (in comparison with other men's ways) hath ever clung to me: and therefore did the hermit (for neither he nor I knew my right name) ever call me Simplicissimus" (p. 20).[43]

The corrupt chaos of the world soon shatters Simplicissimus' innocence and stability. The hermit dies, and in dying he advises Simplicissimus to "know one-self: to avoid bad company: and to stand steadfast" (p. 25).[44] But soon the corrupting force of time does its work and Simplicissimus begins to lose his grief and sense "of my steadfast purpose within." He begins "to falter." He is "overcome by the desire to see the world" (p. 27). Already the forces of instability are at work. The warfare and cruelty that he first sees (p. 28) persuade him the forest (symbol of steadfast purpose and mind) is better than man's world, but the evil rapine of the world drives him at last even out of the forest into the chaos of the world.

There he soon learns roguery. He is sucked into the world in simple ways at first: for example, by enjoying his first good meal. Ironically, the pastor, from whom he should expect further exhortations to stand firm, criticizes the asceticism of Simplicissimus' hermit mentor: "he had been seduced thereto by his reading of many Popish books concerning the lives of ancient eremites" (pp. 47-48).[45] Simplicissimus stands firm at first, condemning the world where he found "naught but vileness," "mere hypocrisy," and "numberless follies" (p. 52).[46] But when he openly criticizes the chaos, he is threatened and learns to acquiesce.[47] The pastor explains that to stand steadfast and speak out would "gain nought . . . but the perilous hatred of these godless fellows." Even the clergy, too worldly wise, helps corrupt the stable and innocent boy into an imitation of the world's trickery.

The sustained assault of trickery, symbol of the world's chaos, begins. First the secretary persuades him "to all manner of folly" (p. 63). Simplicissimus follows this by pulling off a trick, stealing the eyes of a roasted calf (p. 64). He learns from this rather innocent trick that trickery is what the world commends and appreciates: "the gentlemen . . . spoke of my deed, which I had done for pure simplicity, as a wonderous device and a presage of future boldness and fearless and swift resolution" (p. 65).[48] But the trickery is just beginning. Simplicissimus is tricked by the governor (p. 70) and by the secretary again (p. 71).

At last, the world attempts the ultimate trick—the governor attempts to drive Simplicissimus mad, to make him into a fool.

Ironically, again, it is the pastor who shows him that to survive he must deceive, give up his identity. Speaking of the people who will try to befool Simplicissimus, he advises him, "do thou heed not nor believe not all of which they will strive to persuade thee, and yet so carry thyself as if thou believest all" (p. 82).[49] After he takes this advice, Simplicissimus is committed to roguery. He delights in his abilities, reflecting: "consider thou hast victory enough if thou in thy youth canst deceive three such crafty old hags, with whose help one could catch the devil in the open field: from such beginnings thou mayest hope in thine old age to do yet greater things" (p. 85).[50] The world has done its work. The transformation is completed, the ordeal by fire ended: "I have endured the trial by fire and therein have I been hardened: now will we try which of us two can best trick the other" (p. 87).[51] Thus does Simplicissimus silently address the master who has tried to befool him.

The befooling incident in Simplicissimus has the same pivotal force as similar incidents in other picaresque novels where innocent youths are turned into worldly tricksters. The stone trick by the blind man in *Lazarillo,* the inn tricks in *Guzmán,* the inn and university tricks in *Buscón* all represent the same rite of passage. But though it leads from innocence to maturity, it leads not to real strength but to real weakness. The picaro emerges from the dark night not cleansed, but befouled. And it is wrong to speak as though the character *emerges* from the dark night. Rather, he merely goes on penetrating it further when he joins his forces with the darkened world.

Gil Blas's early experience on the road is typical enough of our novels. He is robbed twice and tricked at an inn and by a muleteer. His parents have advised him to be good and not to deceive anyone, but he soon learns that the world is quite roguish, reflecting: "far from exhorting me not to deceive any one, they ought to have advised me not to allow myself to be deceived" (*1,* 18).[52] He soon falls into the hands of robbers and gets what seem like good picaresque lessons about the universality of deceivers and criminals. The robber captain tells him not to fret about being among robbers:

> Why! Is there any other species of men in the world? No, my friend, all men like to take what belongs to others; it is a general sentiment; the only difference lies in the manner of practicing it. Conquerors, for instance . . . People of quality borrow and never repay. Bankers, treasurers, stock-brokers, clerks, and tradesmen of all kinds, great and small, are not over-scrupulous.

61

As for men of law . . . every one knows what they can do [*1*, 34].[53]

These sentiments, if not the style, might have come from *Guzmán de Alfarache*. They proclaim roguery to be universal, and therefore we expect Gil Blas to join the band of robbers and enter into the universal chaos of deception and lawlessness.

He does indeed join the band of robbers, but he joins in order to escape. Far from embracing the chaos of experience, he sees experience as only partly chaotic and still wishes to remain good and stable. His view is confirmed by the novel. It has its share of rogues, but it is also full of virtuous characters: Seraphina, the Count of Olivarez' wife, Alphonso, his father, and his father-in-law, to mention only a few.

Gil Blas himself stands somewhere between the poles formed by the roguish and the virtuous. In the first two-thirds of the book, he is certainly much closer to the honest men than to the rogues. When he sinks as low as he will ever get, among the immoral actresses (*1*, 261 ff.), it is only a momentary lapse into a type of roguery, lasting a brief "three weeks" and taking only ten pages to recount (*1*, 261-71). Then, stung by conscience, he leaves the actresses. As late as 2, 238, he is characterized by Count Galiano as "a very honest young man," and albeit he has done some shady things, we are willing to accept this characterization as largely true. Though he becomes a real rogue at the court, he soon reverts to his non-roguish character. His career as cynical seller of offices and royal favors lasts a scant sixty-five pages (*3*, 34-99). His imprisonment ends his chaos of character in regard to roguery, as in the other aspects we shall examine. One hundred pages after the beginning of his real picaresque career he says: "I intended, if ever I should get out of prison, to buy a cottage, and live there like a philosopher" (*3*, 132).[54]

In Le Sage's satiric vision, *picardía,* trickery, and thievery are not necessary, but only possible alternatives to existence. Men can be honest, e.g., honest servants, and get along. The world is only partly chaotic, partly roguish, and a man can choose and live a stable, honest life in the stable, honest part.

Moll Flanders' seduction by the elder son of the middle-class family she stays with begins her picaresque education. She is vain and prideful, but she does love the elder brother rather selflessly. This openness and honesty are radically changed by a seduction in which all society participates. Not only is the upper-middle-class elder brother involved, a Sir W——— H——— helps by furnishing a carriage to take her away, and yet another man, "confidant" of the brother, helps by furnishing the "certain place" where the physical seduction actually takes place (pp. 22-23). In addition to taking her virtue in a technical sense, the elder brother teaches her that money is all that counts and that she can get money by using her femininity. From this experience Moll also learns to lie. The elder brother maneuvers her into bed by promising her love and marriage before her fall. Afterward he forgets these promises. Trying to maneuver him into marriage and love, Moll tells her first lies.

The elder brother further participates in her corruption by urging her to marry the younger brother as the most expedient course for a girl in her situation: "I gave him a look full of horror at those words . . ." (p. 33). Gradually her outrage at the proposal is dissipated: the pressure of her lonely social situation, the betrayal by the elder brother and his corrupting arguments win out at last. Moll goes through a time of sickness and comes out of this version of the picaresque rite of passage able to meet the roguish world that has corrupted her. She consents to marry a man she doesn't love, to give up "love" for "interest," to pass from being a passionate and pure lover to being a deceiving calculator. She gives up her self for "interest."

In its treatment of roguery, *Roderick Random* differs somewhat from our other picaresque novels. There is no doubt that Roderick and Smollett view the world as full of roguery. Roderick is mistreated by his family and by Potion the pharmacist. He is tricked in London both gratuitously and for his money (*1*, 84 *et passim*), tricked and mistreated by Gawky and his wife, by Mackshane and Oakum, by Crampley and his men, and so forth. Smollett announces that he writes his book exactly to discover the "sordid and vicious disposition" of the world (*1*, xli), and Roderick Random finds the world as Smollett describes it. In the middle of the novel, Roderick compares himself to his uncle Bowling, saying he is "better acquainted [than his uncle] with the selfishness and roguery of mankind, [and] consequently less liable to disappointment and imposition" (*2*, 161). In his experience of universal roguery, then, Roderick's life *is* typical of the picaresque novel.

But if Roderick experiences a picaresque education in discovering the universality of roguery, he reacts by only partially, or intermittently, becoming a rogue himself. Considered from the point of view of the picaresque education, *Roderick Random* is strangely contradictory. If mankind is as bad as he and Smollett say, it is contradictory that Roderick should remain a non-rogue almost alone among mankind. One may speculate that a certain egotism in Smollett's own character caused the mistake. He seems to have thought of himself as a uniquely good man trapped in an evil and hostile world, and he may have projected this implausible vision in his non-roguish hero's confrontation with a roguish world. Whatever the reason for Smollett's mistake, the implausible fracture in both vision and characterization is there in the novel.

We may conveniently describe the incoherence that so many readers have found in the novel by saying that Smollett never decided whether he was writing a picaresque novel, a melodrama, or a moral comedy. Roderick does become a rogue, for a time, when he tries to be a fortune hunter. On the other hand, his picaresque role is slight because Smollett must keep the hero pure in order to show a good man severely oppressed (melodrama). Moreover, since Smollett wants to end on a joyful, comic note, Roderick's career is sometimes described as a typical initiation into a world both good and bad. His father is described as having "blessed God for the adversity I [Roderick] had undergone, which, he said, enlarged the understanding, improved the heart, steeled the constitution, and qualified a young man for all the duties and enjoyments of life, much better than any education which affluence could bestow" (3, 188).

The world in which such a statement is true is not inherently roguish, but merely tainted with "adversity." Sometimes the world is painted all bad, sometimes good and bad. Roderick is a picaro here, a long-suffering saint elsewhere, and in some places just an average youth involved in an average initiation to average experience. The confusion in the book's treatment of Roderick's roguery is symptomatic of its general confusion in device and therefore in vision. Most readers have agreed, however, that the picaresque parts of the novel are more convincing than the others and help make the book a success, though an imperfect one.

Only some of Lazarillo's tricks are devised to meet the world's trickery and better his position. He fights the blind man, for example, often at considerable cost to himself, because the blind man represents the system that abuses him:

> I began to lead him down the worst roads possible—and on purpose, in order to hurt him and endanger him. If there were stones ahead, we went that way; if there was mud we went through the deepest part of it; and although I did not emerge from it as dry-shod as I might have liked, I would have been

perfectly happy to lose one of my own eyes if I could have caused him to lose both of his—if he had had any to lose [p. 35].[55]

Hitting back is a most sincere but also a most primitive action. In such a scream at reality the picaro's voice emerges strong, but not clear. It fights chaos with a chaotic utterance, but with nothing more. If the picaro seems to some extent the anarchist as frustrated idealist, then his cry of pain does not argue for a self more ordered than anarchy. Here we have a significant paradox: the voices of the picaros who tell these tales are strong, but the personalities behind them are so disordered as to be almost nonexistent. Even in the moments when his being cries out, the picaro is without an organized self.

Guzmán de Alfarache not only becomes a gratuitous trickster, but, like Lazarillo, he joins a society of such tricksters—he joins an underworld that preys on the overworld while it reflects the chaotic image of the overworld. The underworld society motif is an old one, but in *Guzmán* it is used with particularly shrewd effect. For one thing, this underworld society not only reflects the roguery of the overworld (already painted with some detail in the novel), but it criticizes that overworld by exhibiting an order within disorder, a stability within instability, that the overworld can never attain. The tricksters or beggars he joins are bound by law and order. *They* never trick their fellow tricksters or infringe on their rights. All is carefully regulated—dress, membership, defense, government, entertainment, seniority, working hours, and so on—by the "Lawes and Ordinances, that are inviolably to be observed amongst Beggars" (2, 147).[56] By overturning society's rules, the beggars attain a state of existence better than the one society offers. Thus, all beggars are forbidden to work: "For their gaines will be little, and their labour much . . ." (p. 153). Since society is a chaos, a better life may be led outside society in embracing *pure* chaos. People in society are constantly striving for stability, riches, honor, security. Since society is chaotic, it constantly frustrates these drives. The only logical thing to do then is to embrace pure chaos in trickery and not try for the usual stability. The world of beggary is revealed as a kind of pastoral Utopia: more efficient, natural, and satisfying than the overworld.[57]

In this underworld, trickery is an art. Guzmán conquers reality through this art. He goes out begging in the siesta hour merely "out of curiositie" to see what art can do under adverse conditions. When hot water is thrown on him, he does not allow himself to be defeated, but bounces back with invention: "grievously complaining, that I was kill'd by some of that house." The result is that the world's trick on him is turned to his own advantage and Guzmán is pitied by others who are not party to his confidence: "True it is, that I was scalded, but not in that cruell manner as I made my crimination" (2, 158).[58]

But when Guzmán goes to school to one of the foremost artists and learns the art, like any good artist he also learns to be impersonal. The ultimate result of Guzmán's roguery, both the earlier directed kind and the later nondirected kind, is the disappearance of his personality. In his roguish career as beggar, he literally gives up his self. He is told by his elder tutor-in-roguery such things as "Answere evill language, with milde words, and to rough speech, apply soft tearmes . . ." (2, 162).[59] The personality of the picaresque hero is completely suppressed in his rogery; he becomes a mere chaos of appearances: "Besides all this, he taught me how to faigne my selfe a Leper, to make wounds in my flesh, to raise a swelling in my legge, to benumme an arme, to set a counterfeit colour on the face, to alter the whole body, and other curious principles of his Art" (2, 162).[60] All that seems to exist under these appearances is a single-minded will to trickery: art for art's sake.

The addition of the art theme makes picaresque trickery not quite the same in *Guzmán* as in *Lazarillo*. Trickery in *Guzmán* is truly non-directional. Neither a howl of pain at the world's way nor a revenge on the world, it is a mere rehearsal of the way of the world—a hyperbolic reflection. Even after Guzmán leaves the ranks of the beggars, he remains an inveterate non-directive trickster. When he is at the cardinal's house, he explains that not what is gained by a trick, but the trick itself, is the thing. If a box of conserves were easy to open, "I would not care a button for them, there is no pleasure in such a purchase. In matters of difficultie, your good wits come to their tryall . . . not in . . . things easie to be done, and which naturally offer themselves unto us at the first sight" (2, 238).[61] The commitment to pure trickery is one way in which the picaro's character reflects the same chaotic image of the world, the same sense of chaos, that the plot does.

The same pattern is Pablos' in *El Buscón*. His picaresque education having been completed on his entrance to the university, he also becomes a gratuitous trickster. Some of the tricks described in the sixth chapter gain him food or money, but others are merely gratuitous. When the housekeeper becomes wise to his tricks, he does not search for a new victim to exploit financially but a new object to divert him: "Since I was now in the bad graces of the housekeeper and could not put anything over on her, I had to look elsewhere for means of amusing myself . . ." (p. 122).[62] The subsequent thefts at the confectionery shop are largely gratuitous. Like Guzmán, Pablos rejoices in the art of trickery for its own sake. When he hears himself praised for his skill in accomplishing some daring tricks (pp. 123-24), he resolves to try more tricks. The theft of the night-watch's swords together with the deception of the president of the university and the police (pp. 124-26) shows Pablos a *magister ludi*. Abdicating personality to become a pure trickster, he endorses the world's madness by becoming mad himself.

This is even more true of his later adventures in Madrid. Pablos' tricks at the university might well have been explained as mere youthful good spirits, but the senseless trickery he performs as a member of the fake-gentleman-beggar-thief circle betrays Pablos' true derangement. It is the same mad underworld-pastoral society that we saw in *Guzmán*: a society run by rule in order to perform tricks for their own sake. Pablos has no need to join the band; he has money to make some other start, but he does join. He observes the rules, giving up his own good clothes to put on the shreds and patches of men whose life is deception. Progressively he immerses himself in a world of appearances. The patched finery of the thieves conceals their poverty and immorality and serves as a telling metaphor for the patchwork chaos of appearances that the picaresque novel represents reality to be.

Simplicissimus is also partly gratuitous in his trickery. In reading through the long and painful tale of his corruption into roguery, we are prepared for his trying to revenge himself on the world. As the wise, invulnerable fool, Simplicissimus revenges himself on reality in chilling satire, criticizing the social injustice of inherited nobility, the stupidity of war, the arts of men ("vanities and follies"), and the institutions of the corrupt and chaotic world. Perhaps his tone seems more bitter because we realize he knows his own life is also chaos. He knows life is bad, but since he can't escape it, he joins it. In his struggles with life's disorder, we watch the bitter gestures of an angry and disordered mind.

His gratuitous roguery is a revenge; it is also an art. Like Guzmán and Pablos, Simplicissimus delights in roguery for its own sake. Though this too is felt in some way by the reader as a revenge on experience, it may be isolated from more purposeful revenge. The delight in trickery is evident from Simplicissimus' first becoming a fool, but only strikes a dominant note when he becomes the Huntsman of Soest. Here the picaro exults in his mastery of experience—in his ability to oppose the chaos he brings to the chaos he finds. The breathless delight in his own sufficiency is evident on every page in which he tells his adventures: "And so did I everywhere, and gained much fame"; "I had sought and found honour, fame and favour in deeds which in others had deserved punishment"; "I was so busied to gain honour and fame that I could not sleep by reason of it, and being full of such fancies, and lying awake many a night to devise new plots and plans . . ." (pp. 161-63).[63] Here is an addled brain indeed—a trickster *par excellence*—another encourager and symbol of the world's chaotic ways. Feverishly in action, feverishly inventing new tricks for no good aim, Simplicissimus has given his mind over to autotelic and senseless activity.

This process never occurs in Gil Blas, because, as we have said, he never gives himself over to roguery. Gil Blas spends practically all his life as a servant or steward or secretary, he never joins or leads a band of beggars or raiders, and he never plays tricks for their own sake.

There is, however, an interesting vestige of gratuitous trickery in Le Sage's novel. When Gil Blas falls into the hands of the forest robbers early in his career (Book I, Chapter v), he is invited to join their subculture. Like the beggar culture in *Guzmán,* the robber life is painted as better than established society. The cook tells Gil Blas he should "rejoice at being here. You are young, and you seem simple; you would soon have been ruined in the world. You would certainly have met with libertines who would have drawn you into all kinds of excesses, whilst here your innocence is in a safe haven" (*1,* 35).[64] But the proposition that the thieves' world is more satisfying than the social world, which has such devastating ironic force in *Guzmán,* is here rejected as false. Gil Blas refuses to become a rogue, refuses to be a professional trickster, because the world outside has room for the good and the stable. Good and stable, in this and other regards, he remains.

Neither does Moll Flanders trick quite gratuitously. She is always interested in securing a stable situation, in getting enough money to live comfortably, always until near the end. But though she never becomes a gratuitous thief, she does become a compulsive one. She must always have more money. Even when her "governess" in crime urges her to stop and insists that Moll has enough, Moll confesses: "I could not forbear going abroad again" (p. 261). Whether her habit is due to having become accustomed to thievery or having become accustomed to accumulating wealth is never quite clear. Certainly, we are meant to feel that here is a person, whatever the motivation, who has become deeply corrupted, who is a rogue per se, and who can't help being one.

We might plausibly also read behind the bare intentions of the novel and say that part of Moll's compulsive trickery is due to an anxiety about gaining ever more money that her society has built into her. If life is as precarious as the Fortune pattern suggests, if Moll's particular social position is so precarious, if the world is full of threatening rogues and also of the underworld, and if money is what everyone looks to for stability, then Moll, in her compulsive roguery, is nothing but a parody of early capitalistic society: a group of rogues whose lives are largely subordinated to the impulse to secure money by any means. Not merely Moll's directed roguery, but also her chaotic, compulsive roguery is the product and reflection of a chaotic world whose products are the deranged—compulsive tricksters and money-grabbers who have forgotten the purpose of trickery and money. It is a world where trickery ultimately becomes autotelic because trickery is its basic stuff and expression. Moll's England is merely another version of the picaresque world.

IV

Protean Form

T HE CONFUSION OF the picaro's personality is revealed in the protean forms he assumes. There is no part that the picaro will not play. Typically, he can turn his hand to anything, assume the social disguise of every profession and vocation. Lazarillo, for example, is a servant, an altar boy, a beggar's boy, a constable's man, a water-seller, a wine-seller, a town crier, and so forth. In his tricks he assumes still other guises. At the priest's house he disguises his behavior in robbing the chest by pretending to be both a mouse and a snake. And he is capable of even more amazing and grotesque feats of self-alteration: "It so happened that during my stay with the blind man I had transformed my mouth into a purse, and I could often keep the equivalent of twelve or fifteen maravedís—in little coins—in my mouth without being inconvenienced while I ate. Otherwise, I should never have possessed a farthing of my own without the blind man's spotting it . . ." (p. 51).[65] In his protean guises, the picaro's character becomes, once more, radically undefined. He assumes whatever appearance the world forces on him, and this a-personality is typical of the picaresque world, in which appearance and reality constantly mingle, making definition and order disappear.

In the end, the character of the picaro may sometimes disappear entirely behind a mask. This is the final brilliant stroke of *Lazarillo*. Lazarillo, who has assumed so many forms, put on so many disguises, and told so many lies, in the end lies to us. He never admits that the cause of his new and final prosperity is a *ménage á trois;* he

70

denies it stoutly. In this first picaresque novel, we see and feel the
character whom we have trusted as narrator and sympathized with
as actor betray us at last. Even the fragments of Lazarillo's personality have dissolved. He has become to us and to his world sheer appearance, a living lie. But this final disappearance of personality is
unique in the novels we are considering: usually, the picaro finishes
by being as chaotic as ever, only more tired.

Guzmán de Alfarache is typical in his protean forms. There is
nothing he does not do and cannot do. Sayavedra sums up some of
the picaro's transformations in telling his own story ("I was of all
occupations; a mariner, a miller, a baker, a scout, a crosse-biter, one
of your upright men, a cheater, a cozener, a fox, that was full of
craft and subtletie . . ." (3, 266).[66] In his protean changes, the picaro
again reveals that the world is in chaos. It demands new things, new
guises of a man all the time. The pressures of society, Fortune, and
accident never let a character rest in a single posture.

On the other hand, viewed solely as a character, the picaro reveals
in his variability his abdication of self-determination. If society is
a chaos of appearances, he will embrace that chaos by becoming
totally "other-directed." There are other choices open to him, of
course: death, suffering, and suicide. But since the picaro's one
constant trait is his will to live, he will live any way he can. Guzmán
declares his other-directed lack of personality in several places:
"Mine eie was not set upon my selfe, but on others; and looke what
I saw them doe, that (me thought) was likewise lawfull for me
. . ." (2, 48).[67] "I was continually carefull in seeking out that, which
to that office which I now professed [Jester], was necessarily required, that I might still goe getting of ground, and accommodate
other mens taste to mine owne" (3, 45-46).[68] At one point, Guzmán
refers to himself as an "instrument" of his master. He will subordinate his personality, because the world doesn't want it. He realizes
that the world runs by appearances: "Men doe judge now more by
the eye, then the eare . . . the outside is more looked on, then the
inside looked into . . ." (3, 344).[69]

From other literature we have come to expect limits to adaptability, limits to the extent a character will sacrifice his personality. But
in the picaresque there are no limits. The picaro is every man he has
to be, and therefore no man. If we draw a continuum of personality
from single-minded integrity to adaptable multiplicity, we shall find
that most people, and most characters in the realistic novel, fall
somewhere in the middle. Most of us have some personality as well
as some lack of it, if we define the lack of personality (albeit

71

somewhat arbitrarily) as the ability to adapt to changing circumstances by changing the self. As the infinitely adaptable man, however, the picaro sits on the pole furthest from integrity. In his total chaos of personality, he speaks to us of the grimmer aspects of our own lives. He speaks of the thousand daily compromises we make with reality, of our lack of true inner stability, our lack of self, our lack of heroism.

Critics may claim that the totally other-directed picaro is a symbolic *exaggeration* of people in real life. He only represents, they might say, one end of the continuum between integrity and adaptability, and therefore is not "true" to life as a whole. But much the same objection could be made for the tragic hero. How many of us, like the tragic hero or the saint, are willing to take our duty, our sense of personal worth, even our failure, as seriously as Hamlet, Othello, or Sophocles' Ajax? How many of us are willing to die, to kill ourselves, lest we live a lowered mode of existence, lest we sacrifice part of our true being?

Yet as we respond with mingled joy and tears to the defeat/victory [70] of the tragic hero, so we respond with anxiety and sympathy to the total chaos of the protean picaro. As each of us can approach in small ways a tragic integrity in our lives, so each of us does approach, I suspect in more than small ways, a picaresque lack of integrity. The picaresque novel does not give us the joy and courage of tragedy, often called the highest genre. The picaresque novel is ugly; it speaks of the possibilities of human degradation rather than of human triumph. Yet it is just as "true" to experience.

Were a moralist like F. R. Leavis to say that the picaresque novel "does dirt on life," one would have to reply that it merely reveals the endless real possibilities of life's dirt. If we were to quiet the moralist, we might say, not that the picaresque novel is a caution to us, but that it is a protest against men as they are and as the world causes them to be. Behind the narrator of each picaresque novel we feel the moralistic implied author [71] shrieking hate at the world's and men's chaos, shrieking in rage at what the world has done to him personally. Such cries may be immature, may be unresolved art, inferior to the transcendent synthesis of great comedy, for example, in which the conflict between the real and the ideal is magically and momentarily resolved.[72] But wherever it fits into the hierarchy of literary art forms, the picaresque novel in its radically other-directed protagonist has a compelling truth that cannot be denied.

Everywhere, picaresque novels are a criticism of life. Just as Pablos, el Buscón, is chaotic in his origins, in his feelings, and in his roguery, so he is chaotic in his many social masks. His story has a greater apparent unity than most picaresque stories because he is continually posing as, and wishing to be, a rich nobleman. But he also assumes many other disguises. At the end, Pablos abandons his aspirations to rise and plunges into whatever comes his way, becoming in turn an actor, poet, wooer of nuns, and strong-arm tough, all within thirty pages (pp. 204-33). This astonishing adaptability serves as an appropriate climax to the development of the picaro's character. Before we had something of the impression of a character with a more or less fixed ideal, trying to realize that ideal. We had an impression of a certain amount of personality organization. Now we have only the impression of complete plasticity. Now the picaro no longer attempts to move life from a set ideal within himself; instead he moves with life, becoming what life asks of him at each moment. Pablos' final hint that things did not change for him when he went to America makes us believe that the process of character disintegration is just beginning. The continuation, it is suggested at the end of what Quevedo has left us, would show a character more protean, more chaotic than ever.

Simplicissimus also gradually falls from steadfastness to other-directed adaptability.[73] The good pastor, whose role in Simplicissimus' picaresque education is described above, also teaches him the skill of trimming his sails to the prevailing winds. By his own example, he teaches Simplicissimus the ways of adjustment. When Simplicissimus is in trouble after the goose-pen incident, he goes to the pastor for advice and help. But the man who has ridden into favor on Simplicissimus' coattails betrays his benefactor now that the situation has changed: "Get thee quick out of bed and pack out of my house, lest I come with thee under my lord's displeasure if thou be found here with me" (p. 75).[74]

Soon after this incident, Simplicissimus, partly exonerated of the charge of tricking the Governor of Hanau, is able to learn such protean trimming from all of society. When the Swedish Commissary comes to inspect Hanau, everyone in town puts on a face. Even the governor, formerly seen as stable and inviolate in his commanding position, is shown embodying the flexibility and betrayal of integrity that typifies the picaresque world: "he wished, he said, the devil had broke his [the Commissary's] neck in a thousand pieces ere ever he came to the city. Yet so soon as he had let him in and welcomed him upon the inner drawbridge it wanted but a little, or nothing at all, but he would hold his stirrup for him to shew his devotion . . ." (p. 80).[75] From this little exhibition, Simplicissimus learns, as he says, "what a wondrous spirit of falsehood doth govern all mankind" (p. 80).[76]

From now on, there is no form Simplicissimus will not assume in order to live. When the world forces the appearance of a calf (!) on Simplicissimus, he assumes it. Captured by the Croats, he is forced to be a jester, groom, and cook; he bows to the pressure to become protean. When he is on his own, without food, he yields to necessity and becomes a thief. At one point, he even "becomes" a woman, boiling, baking, and washing while disguised in a dress. His adaptability, then, is absolute, but still he has not mastered the world. He is essentially a reacting agent. When circumstances change, he changes his personality and behavior to suit them. The picaresque hero is active in his personal chaos as rogue, essentially passive as protean character. As rogue, he adds to the world's chaos and fights it; as protean character, he merely swims with the stream of events.

His whole life becomes pretenses and appearances. Though prideful, he says of his demeanor as a prisoner, "I shewed myself as modest as might be" (p. 206).[77] By suiting his words and actions to each person in the town, he gains favor and protects himself. There is in the picaro an almost paranoid fear. He seems to have learned from sad experience that the fluctuations of Fortune are so great that one must hedge against them. He becomes all things to all men, lest anyone be minded to turn against him, telling us he took "care to keep all men's affection so long as I was minded to sojourn in that fortress" (p. 219).[78] He lies, he gives gifts, he holds banquets, he even makes it his business to placate the local pastor, since religious authorities are respected (p. 220). We see him playing one part after another, desperately trying to adjust to the world, until, finally, he decides to leave the disorder of the world and the disorder it requires of personality to become a steadfast isolate like his true father.[79]

Gil Blas differs from this character pattern just as it differs from the others discussed. In the first place, Gil is allowed to play much smaller a variety of roles than other picaros. They, as we have seen, are much more than *mozos de muchos amos* (as traditional criticism maintained), but Gil Blas is not. It is true he becomes a quack doctor for a while and joins the theater briefly. But these and similar episodes are as nothing compared with the overwhelming majority of the narrative, in which he plays the single role of servant. Even as a doctor, he is in a subordinate position as helper and assistant to Dr. Sangrado. He shows little of the free-floating variation of professional roles that a true picaro such as Simplicissimus does. He is always the able assistant, a man who can carry out orders, not a

Huntsman of Soest, an engineer, a general of sixty thousand troops, a hermit, a dark voyage adventurer, like Simplicissimus. Simplicissimus assumes the changing forms of a picaresque world; Gil Blas retains his own form in a relatively stable, non-picaresque world.

Still, if we overlook his professional stability, Gil Blas does exhibit much of the other-directed lack of integrity of the true picaresque hero. Like him, Gil Blas is able to put on a face to meet the faces that he meets. For example, he is able to flatter the Archbishop of Granada outrageously and to feign admiration and affection for him (2, 248-49). On the other hand, he has enough integrity to be "open and sincere" in criticism of the Archbishop's sermons when they become bad. He realizes this may be a mistake in prudence, but Gil cannot seem to resist fulfilling the terms of his compact with the Archbishop to criticize him when his sermons do become bad. It is part of his faithful servant role. Thus, Gil Blas is protean and integral by turns. We might think of such a character as rather realistic. This indeed is the way most of us are: trimming here and being ourselves there. But such is not the vision of most of our classic picaresque novels.

If Gil Blas is no more protean than a good-humored, comic adjuster-to-circumstances during most of the book, he becomes truly protean in the one hundred pages in which he also becomes truly roguish. At the court, every vestige of integrity goes. Once Gil Blas leaves the court, however, he soon ceases to be protean, and he reverts to a comic adjusting to circumstances without sacrificing his integrity. He goes along with Dr. Sangrado's inveighing against the new medical science: "However much I was disposed to laugh on hearing such a comical outburst, I succeeded in restraining my merriment; nay, more, I inveighed against *kermes* without knowing what it meant, and, at all risks, sent to the deuce those who had invented it" (3, 149).[80] The true sacrifice of personality, which we see in the book's brief picaresque section (3, 3-99), has become a slight masking of personality for the sake of politeness and quiet comic amusement at the foolish doctor. Gil may change his guise again, as when he becomes a pamphleteer for Olivarez and a tutor to his son. He may suit his style of writing to his master's ideas, even if he doesn't believe them (3, 295, 302). But Gil Blas is a protean hero only for the briefest period.

Moll Flanders, because she is an eighteenth-century woman, can be expected to show nothing like the great variation of professional roles of a male picaro. She is like Gil Blas in always playing the one role of wife (or thief), just as he almost always plays the one role of servant. On the other hand, the plasticity of personality implied by being able to marry seven or eight different men (one can never remember the exact number of these husbands) is infinitely greater than that implied by being able to serve many different types of masters.

She refashions her personality to suit the temperament and circumstances of each new husband. The conservative and mild-mannered banker and the wild, exuberant, devil-may-care "gentleman tradesman" both find her perfectly satisfactory because she makes herself so. She transforms herself into whatever the situation requires, and lives with each of these totally different types, intimately and happily, for many years. This important pattern is established early, at the time of her picaresque education. Then she learns to suit the elder brother of the family at Colchester as a mistress, and the younger, more conservative and honest brother as a wife.

When her gentleman tradesman fails in business, she recalls a typical protean maneuver: "the first thing I did was to go quite out of my knowledge, and go by another name" (p. 60). It is not the only time she changes her apparent identity in this fundamental way. After she has shown another woman how to disguise herself as rich, she shows her own mastery of appearances by changing her name again in order to show herself as a rich widow: "I resolved, therefore, that it was necessary to change my station, and make a new appearance in some other place, and even to pass by another name if I found occasion" (p. 73). In addition to these and other later changes of name, we may observe that Moll's real name is unknown even to us: "it is not to be expected I should set my name or the account of my family to this work" (p. 1). All this ambiguity about her name, all these changes of names, demonstrate a deeper protean nature in this character than any mere changes in profession could project.

Moll also shows her uncanny ability to use actual physical disguises. Even early in the book she is able to disguise herself as a serving maid in order to find out about the health of her gentleman lover. But her physical disguises are more frequent in the second part of her career. What appearance is beyond her capacities when she turns thief? She can even change her sex, as did Simplicissimus, disguising herself as a man (p. 220). When the police run after her she rushes into her governess' house, sheds her male disguise, and a few minutes later appears to the constable as a respectable matron: "I had a little girl with me, which was my governess's grandchild, as she called her; and I bade her open the door, and there I sat at work with a great litter of things about me, as if I had been at work all day . . ." (pp. 222-23). Later she takes up "the disguise of a widow's dress" (p. 248) and still later dresses herself "like a beggar woman, in the coarsest and most despicable rags . . ." (p. 261). Though less literally, her demeanor at the novel's end may also be thought of as a disguise, and she continues to conceal parts of her identity even from her Lancashire husband and her beloved son.

Roderick Random, on the other hand, exhibits the same contradictoriness in this aspect of his character as in others. Sometimes he is a protean disguiser and adjuster to circumstances, and sometimes he is the adamant, inner-directed romance hero. Like most picaros, he embraces a variety of professions: doctor, apothecary, soldier, sailor, fortune-hunter, merchant, servant. Like most picaros, he is well able to dissemble, to suit his demeanor to the occasion, as, for example, when he flatters Narcissa's poetess aunt, or when he tries to adjust to the miserable fate of being pressed aboard Oakum's ship (2, 36).

But there is another strain in Roderick's character, a strain arising from his aristocratic birth, that identifies him with romance heroes. If sometimes he bows and adjusts to circumstances like a true picaro, at other times he takes arms against them in the name of his pride, honor, and resentment. On page 35 of Volume II, he resolves in protean fashion to make the best of being pressed aboard the *Thunder,* but on page 36 of the same volume he treats the insolent midshipman Crampley pridefully. When Crampley asks who has removed his manacles, Roderick answers: "Whoever did it, I am persuaded did not consult you in the affair." This daring, haughty, and courageous reflex bespeaks the conventional romance hero, not the typical picaro we have come to know.

V

Loneliness and Love

HE EMOTION OF LOVE
and the sentiment of loyalty, which help so much to order and focus
our psychic lives, are so curiously absent in the picaresque novel as to
deserve specific but brief treatment in any consideration of the
picaresque character. As a result of his lack of love, the picaresque
hero attains a loneliness that is oddly similar to that of some tragic
heroes. But tragic heroes are lonely to an end. They raise themselves
far above ordinary men in order to complete a necessary task. Their
loneliness is, thus, a measure of their single-mindedness, of the
organization of their emotion. The picaro, on the other hand, has no
fixed emotional position toward anyone or anything. His lack of
love expresses a lack of personality. This lack of integrity, of internal
order, symbolically reflects a disorder in the world, and it is also a
practical reaction to that disorder. If things are chaotic outside, one
cannot practically attach oneself to any person or thing; Fortune
will blast all attachments, or other men will be revealed as unable to
reciprocate love. As we have seen in connection with the picaresque
education, the unanchored self (or non-self) is the only possible self
in such a world. The blind beggar promises to accept Lazarillo "not
as a servant but as his son" (p. 29).[81] But there is really no question
of love involved. The blind man does not want to organize his inner
life or Lazarillo's around a stability such as love, but rather to reduce
Lazarillo to a state of utter non-being as the pure instrument of his
will. The promise of paternal love is broken by the slap of Lazarillo's head against the stone animal. Lazarillo first reacts by discover-

ing his true loneliness in the world: "I am on my own" (p. 30).[82] He
then affirms the social disorder of the world by revenging himself on
the blind man and promptly forgetting about him. He leaves the
blind man unconscious before the stone pillar, remarking, "I never
learned what happened to the blind man after that; nor did I ever
bother to find out" (p. 41).[83]

To say, however, that Lazarillo never feels anything for anyone
would be wrong. Lack of feeling is his normal condition, but
affections of variously disinterested sorts develop in the book. There
is the surprising and touching affection that he feels for his hidalgo
master: "However, because he had absolutely nothing and no choice,
I had a fond fellow-feeling for him. I felt pity for him . . ." (p.
64).[84] But unfortunately this love is a mere gesture in the direction
of human solidarity. It is based on pity, on a certain feeling for
comradeship in suffering, but it is scarcely an emotional attachment
that organizes the picaro's psyche or behavior in any deep or lasting
way. For the picaro has little or no sentimental memory, no regret
for friends or loved ones lost. The fact that the picaro is not always
cold makes him more sympathetic, but puts his more usual and
fundamental disorganization of personality into bleak relief.

Jack Wilton, in *The Unfortunate Traveller,* typifies the usual
pattern in regard to love and loneliness. Though he is one of the
more lovable picaros, he does not love. Rather, he flirts with emotional attachments. He refers to Surrey as "him I so much adored"
(p. 232), but a non-emotional motivation complicating this attachment is found in Jack's admission: "I was not altogether unwilling
to walk along with such a good purse-bearer . . ." (p. 232).

Throughout, Surrey is satirized as a man who tries to attain *too
much* order and integrity by loving, and who continually fails in his
attempts. Jack's uncommitted emotions are held up as more suited to
the disorder of men's personalities and the anarchy that exists
around them. Surrey is the pure and perfect lover of the "celestial
Geraldine," but when Diamante is thrown into prison with Jack and
him, Surrey feels a sexual attraction to her. His virtue and his love
for Geraldine inhibit any disordered actions that would indicate
disorder of personality. Still, his integrity is not perfect, and his
virtue and devotion to Geraldine finally emerge as an ill-fitting
mask for the chaos of his real sexual desires: "This was all the injury
he would offer her: sometimes he would imagine her in a melan-
choly humor to be his Geraldine, and court her in terms correspond-
ent; nay, he would swear she was his Geraldine, and take her white
hand and wipe his eyes with it . . ." (p. 249).

For Jack, of course, all this is a ridiculous attempt to impose an aprioristic system on life.[85] Since life is not ordered, inside a person or out, one acts, one does not think or feel: "My master beat the bush and kept a coil and a prattling, but I caught the bird" (p. 250). Jack sleeps with Diamante. Attempting to order his inner life through love, Surrey is as disordered as Jack himself, and, what is more, he is comic in not giving in to and affirming the disorder of personality in the picaresque world.

Another example from *The Unfortunate Traveller* is worth mentioning. When Diamante is carried off by Esdras of Granada and his villainous colleague Bartol (p. 272), Jack threatens and cajoles Bartol. His words are the show of true love: "Save her, kill me, and I'll ransom her with a thousand ducats" (p. 272). But when Bartol leaves, Jack's hidden cowardice emerges to expose these words as a mere show of selflessness: "Then threw I myself pensive again on my pallet, and dared all the devils in hell, now I was alone, to come and fight with me one after another in defense of that detestable rape" (p. 272). The fluidity and chaos of Jack's personality contrast with the perfect organizations of the other personalities in this scene: the pure villain Esdras and the virtuous Heraclide. But they are parodies of literary types, and therefore unreal. Esdras' fearful and improbable statistics make him seem fictional: "This is the eightscore house . . . that hath done homage unto me, & here I will prevail, or I will be torn in pieces" (p. 272). And the pure and virtuous Heraclide speaks the fake rhetoric of the abused lady: "No blessing is beauty, but a curse: cursed be the time that ever I was begotten; cursed be the time that my mother brought me forth to tempt" (p. 277). Both are satirized as stock types of literature.

In the book's chaotic world, Jack's chaotic character emerges as the most convincing, the most true to life. Since to be ordered means disaster (Heraclide commits suicide, Esdras is hanged) or frustration (Surrey is a romantic butt), he takes what comes and changes with the world. Jack's Diamante betrays him ("I saw my courtezan kissing very lovingly with a prentice"), and he is at first outraged at her faithlessness (p. 286). But when they both immediately encounter dangers through Zadoch, Zachery, and Juliana, he learns once again that there is no room for finer feelings in such a world. Therefore, Jack eventually takes Diamante back and even marries her in his final show of piety, with no questions asked. But where the marriage of two such faithless and disordered characters will end, the reader may well inquire.

Guzmán de Alfarache's early experiences show the isolation of the picaro. He leaves his mother early, and in the course of his travels comes to Genoa to visit his relatives, but they reject him because he has no money. Where Guzmán should most expect support in his loneliness, he finds persecution. Even the ties between people that *do* develop in *Guzmán* generate a feeling of instability and chaos because they are impermanent. We have discussed, in considering plot, the easy disappearance of characters whom the picaro meets. The instability of human relationships and the loneliness of the picaro are pointedly brought home in the repeated dissolution of picaresque societies. The societal dissolution which ends the first volume of Mabbe's edition,[86] for example, is the very parody of a comic ending. In comedy, society is reformed and solidly re-formed at the end. In the picaresque, it is totally and repeatedly dissolved.

If Guzmán's loneliness defines the difference between picaresque and comic society, his lack of love defines one significant difference between the picaresque and the romance hero. As we have seen in the plot and pattern section, Ozmin and Daraxa may be operationally defined as lovers. Love, a single definite emotion, is their personality, dictates their every feeling and voluntary action. Romance heroes come across to the reader, therefore, as persons ultimately defined and integral. Guzmán merely flirts with romantic love. He reports he "fell in love at the first sight" of his second wife (*4, 222*). Yet the instability of that love is soon exposed. After a short time, Guzmán betrays his love and his wife by becoming her pimp. Love is dissolved by concern for the material world; in short, the picaro is too busy concentrating on material reality to have a self with which to love.

When we realize the picaro's lack of love, we feel once again that disorder has invaded the personality. Erich Fromm says that "The deepest need of man . . . is the need to overcome his separateness. . . . The *absolute* failure to achieve this aim means insanity. . . ."[87] If the picaro doesn't go insane, in his lonely lack of love, we wonder why. The answer is that as a felt character, he is a person without a stable self. Insanity, as we know it, has little meaning in his picaresque chaos. The picaro's condition of personality is so unstable that it always approaches insanity, thereby reflecting the insane lack of structure of the picaro's world.[88]

Simplicissimus, however, differs from most other picaros in being able to feel genuine affection for other people. He has considerable feeling for his hermit tutor, for the governor of Hanau (p. 204), and especially for Herzbruder. Herzbruder's very name sets him off from most other picaresque sidekicks, who are felt as anything but brothers of the heart by such picaros as Guzmán de Alfarache or Jack Wilton. But because Simplicissimus is in many ways as lonely and unfeeling as other picaros, his apparent difference is only a variation on the usual picaresque pattern.

His loneliness is almost absolute. Even his meetings with Herzbruder are intermittent and infrequent, and Herzbruder dies at last. He early loses both his supposed and real parents, and his should-be foster parent, the pastor, betrays him. He marries twice, but both times his marriage is shattered by separation or death.

Looking more closely at the inward side of his loneliness, we may say that although he loves, he is not a lover. His being is not significantly organized by love except in the final adventures with Herzbruder. Then he does care and is willing to do things and make sacrifices for his friend (pp. 260ff.); but during most of the novel, when Herzbruder is out of sight he is also out of mind. Though Simplicissimus is forced to leave his first wife almost immediately after their marriage, he has virtually no thoughts about her when he is gone. He is fickle in the extreme in his affairs with women, to the extent of becoming a male whore in Paris. In no way can it be said that love or any other emotion organizes his psychic life. In this, he is typical of the non-loving, barren universe into which he has been born. He says, "nowhere did I find more envy, hatred, malice, quarrel, and dispute than between brothers, sisters, and other born friends . . . the handicraftsmen of every place hated one another . . . many a lord would fleece his true servants and subjects and some retainers would play the rogue against the best of lords" (pp. 56–57).[89]

Gil Blas, however, is different from the lonely figures we have seen. His fortunes are constantly being supported by one or another friend or acquaintance; he lives in a world where society is somewhat stable and helps to define the destiny and character of a man; and he can feel love, affection, and sympathy for others. To be sure, we are first struck (*1, 9*) by his ingratitude to the parents and uncle who have raised him. But after this typically picaresque beginning, Gil Blas is shown as a person capable of considerable feeling for others. In the robbers' cave, for example, he feels a humane concern for the captured damsel that almost approaches the tender sensibility of the romance hero. Gil Blas is even willing to venture his safety for this girl he has never seen before. His ability to feel for others is not only a stable trait of his personality and a stabilizing factor in it but also a means of securing friends and preserving him from loneliness.

In his loyalty, tenderness, and lovingness, Gil Blas has moved away from the picaresque character's disorganization in the direction of the stability of the heroes of romance and heroic drama. In his ability to love, Gil Blas again stands in contrast to the true picaros appearing in the novel, who are later punished for their antisocial *picardía* and selfishness just as Gil Blas is rewarded for his goodness and lovingness. When the decadent Laura re-encounters him, she tells Gil that she has turned her back on love: "I want no more an affection which disturbs my peace" (2, 284; Bardon, 2, 38). She views love as disorganizing because her "love" is an immoral and passionate one. Gil Blas's love is non-picaresque in having a strong element of legality and morality.

Now just as every other aspect of Gil Blas's stability of character is briefly disrupted by his behavior as favorite of the Duke of Lerma, so are his love, loyalty, and tenderness. But the picaresque universe Gil Blas endorses in the court episode is not the real universe of the novel, and when he is thrown into prison, he quickly comes to himself and reverts to his former character. He feels immediate, generous good will toward Cogollos, his fellow prisoner, and he is able and willing to be a friend again. The prison adventure reinforces and deepens his capacity for affection. Scipio comes to visit him in prison, and their formerly cynical and commercial relationship, born in the corrupt court world, is transformed into a wonderfully sentimental one (3, 125). Later he returns to his parents and feels and cares for them in a manner contrasting vividly with his earlier ingratitude. Though his first marriage is unfortunate, his wife dying during childbirth, his love survives in grief (3, 270), and for twenty-two years he is unwilling to take another wife. When, at the end of the novel, he does remarry, we leave him enjoying the affections of a second wife and two children, more a good country squire than a conventional picaro. In his love, as in nearly every other aspect of his personality, Gil Blas is different from the heroes of the other classic picaresque novels.

Moll Flanders, however, is lonely. From the very beginning she is isolated. Like other picaros, she is unable to love. But her lack of love is interesting because it is something she is taught by the world. She loves the elder brother "to an extravagance not easy to imagine" (p. 52). But once he gives her up and passes her on to his sweet but emasculated younger brother, Moll has learned her lesson: "I had been tricked once by that cheat called love, but the game was over; I was resolved now to be married or nothing, and to be well married or not at all" (p. 56). Moll's picaresque world has shown her that the inner stability which love gives to the lover may lead to painful disorder when shattered by the pressures of the outside world.

Despite her resolutions of practicality, Moll is able to break through the emotional chaos of her picaresque world and to love again as late as the middle of the book. She calls after her departed Lancashire husband: " 'O Jemmy!' said I, 'come back, come back. I'll give you all I have; I'll beg, I'll starve with you' " (p. 155). This momentary, real and organizing emotional attachment is, however, finally forgotten. Under the assault of the world which has thrice separated her from those she has loved (not to speak of the husbands she has not loved but on whom she was materially dependent), she has learned to be practical and to crush or limit her love. She has some affection for Jemmy at the end, and some for her governess, but in neither can she confide completely (pp. 322-24). Even at its best her personality is torn between the affection she feels and the insecurity that haunts her .

As for Roderick Random, one finds this aspect of his character is as unfortunately confused as the others. Sometimes he is lonely and isolated, exposed like a picaresque atom to the fluctuations of Fortune. On the other hand, sometimes Roderick is supported (like Gil Blas) by many friends with whom he has long-standing relationships or whom he often meets. This profusion of helpful and good friends also allows their oppression by the bad world to extend the book's melodramatic theme. At the end, however, the good unite in being rewarded, just as the bad are punished. The presence of this more or less stable good group allows a hearty comic-romantic ending resembling those of Jane Austen's novels in which a good society, purged of all bad elements, is formed at last. Thus, the confusion in the treatment of Roderick's loneliness gives us picaresque, melodramatic, and comic-romantic strains running not too harmoniously through the novel.

The treatment of love exposes, once again, similar strains in the characterization and in the novel's vision. In the romance phase of his characterization, Roderick loves; in the picaresque phase, he does not. Though the love affair with Narcissa, which occupies much of the second half of the book, is a sterile reworking of the standard romance pattern of love, it nevertheless shows Roderick as a lover, as a person capable of love and even willing to make sacrifices for his love. On the other hand, in much of his love experience before and after he meets Narcissa, Roderick resembles other picaros in his inability to love and in his mercenary and generally instrumental attitude toward love. He goes whoring in London on his first trip, sleeps with Miss Lavement as a gesture of revenge, and pays court to Miss Williams, Miss Snapper, and Melinda in order to secure himself a lucrative marriage. All this is typical of the picaro's inability to love in a world where relationships are short and tenuous and where one must concentrate solely on negotiating that picaresque chaos which is reality.

VI

Internal Instability

HE CHAOTIC NATURE of the picaresque character is revealed more directly than has been indicated so far. True, his protean forms, his inability to love, the circumstances of his origins, and his loneliness all give us a sense of his internal anarchy. But his real lack of settled integrity is revealed most clearly in the instability of his resolves. Most people encounter life, learn from experience, and assume a more or less fixed set of postures toward reality. While we may be able to do this only partially, the picaro is unable to do it at all—not merely because life forces him to assume protean forms, not merely because Fortune whirls him along, but because he is simply unable to keep to a set course. He constantly lets go of the outer stability he finds because he is internally unstable.

Largely because his story is more explicitly introspective, Guzmán is more interesting in this regard than the two picaros who precede him. But what will be said about him is largely true also of Lazarillo and Jack Wilton. He is, for example, unstable in his inability to keep to a prudent course of action. This he sees, rightly enough, as a general disease: "It is mens foolishnesse, and their want of judgement and discretion (as I told you before) that leades them thus along . . . to their destruction . . ." (2, 40).[90] Instead of using his money to bolster his fortunes, Guzmán recklessly spends it: "All that I got, I either plaid it away, or unjustly stole it. I had bought me neither goods nor land with it, neither house, nor cloathes, nor any thing wherewithall to cover me" (2, 64).[91] We watch Guzmán go through elaborate precautions to ensure his safety and fortune only to throw them away. For example, he alters the appearance of some clothing he has bought from a young man lest the latter's relatives, by some totally improbable chance, may find Guzmán and think he has killed and robbed the youth (2, 78-79). But he throws away this elaborately prudential hedge against life's chances when he imprudently squanders his money on the Captain (4, 98ff.). This inconsistency is touching and typical.

As he is unstable in his resolves of prudence, so Guzmán is unstable in his moral resolves. He sees his instability as a universal one: "But a man can doe no more than he can doe. . . . Nor doe I know how it comes to passe, that we desiring to be good, yet we never come to be so; and though we propose it dayly and hourely unto our selves, yet we doe not put it in execution in many yeeres; nay, not in all our life-time are we able to reach unto it" (2, 65-66).[92] Here Guzmán condemns us all to the eternal moral instability that to some extent characterizes all men.[93] As a typical man Guzmán continually fails to achieve an internal moral stability and continually records his failure in such phrases as this: "O, what a brave resolution was this, if it would have held!" (3, 148).[94] "I departed from Rome with a full purpose to become an honest man . . . [but] faith, without workes, is but a dead faith" (3, 206).[95] The romance figures who continually reappear in the frame stories of the novel contrast their perfect constancy to the picaro's moral instability: "But the chaste Dorotea, neither by this Gentlemans good parts, nor the *Teniente's* great power, nor all the passions of other her Lovers, could be moved one jot from her honourable resolution. . . . Against all these assaults, shee show'd herselfe a strong Tower, an inexpungable rocke . . ." (4, 51).[96] Such moral constancy occurs, however, only in the heroes of the interpolated romances. The basic story of the novel, its basic reality, portrays men almost always as morally unstable.

Another aspect of the typical picaro's instability is his curiosity and adventurousness. A sudden impulse, a random quirk, continually leads him into trouble. Guzmán, for example, goes to beg in Gaeta "out of curiositie," leaving the security of Rome only to find out later that he has made a mistake (2, 189).[97] Much the same thing happens when he begs during the siesta hours, "meerely out of curiositie, and no other end else in the world" (2, 158).[98] It is impossible to predict what such a restless character will do next.

An even greater feeling of instability is generated by the picaro's inability to hold to a predetermined course of action. On page 70 of

Mabbe's second volume, Guzmán determines to go to Italy to visit his relatives. But by page 80 he has strayed far enough from this purpose to become a dandy in Spain. Four pages after this, he is once more off the track and on his way to Italy in pursuit of amatory adventure.

A notable pattern is the picaro's inability to stay in a secure position retired from the world's chaos. We may call this the adventure-retirement schism. After Guzmán's first disastrous day out of Seville and his unfortunate run-in with the hostess who has served him nearly live chicks for eggs, Guzmán thinks of "repenting my selfe of my ill advised departure." But instead, he chooses to go on. "But it is, and ever will be the fashion of young fellowes, to cast themselves away headlong, upon their present pleasures, without having an eye, or any regard in the world to their future hurt; or the harme that will follow after" (1, 106).[99] Now the picaro's instinctive desire to keep going is of course *necessary* to keep the plot moving and to lengthen the book. But the fact that he continually thinks of retreating from the world and then returns to embrace it is expressive, perhaps, of a touching faith we all have that the world's chaos will eventually order itself if only we can endure. All of us, like the picaro, constantly feel it is worth going on, even though we should know by now that over the hill is the same troubled reality we have found on this side.

The most affecting instance of this pattern occurs when marriage brings the picaro out of his safe retirement. He has resolved to become a priest in order to find a stable place for himself in society (4, 185-86). For seven years, up to the threshold of ordination, he maintains his resolve by studying diligently at Alcalá. But then he sees a girl, and within a few days the resolution, the labor, and the stability of application are all thrown away. The slightest slip, the missing of one lecture, is enough to do it, so unstable are men in their habits: "wherein to faile, though never so little, more than ordinary, is like to the breaking of a stich in a man's stockin, which if it be not taken up in time, will ravell out all the rest" (4, 218).[100] A few pages later the aspirant priest is a pander for his own wife! Whether because of the world's chances or the picaro's unstable temper, inability to withdraw from the world's disorder is fundamental to the picaresque novel. For the logical end of the picaro's experience of the world's flux should be his withdrawal from it to an internal stability, that is, to a type of monasticism. His failure to withdraw, his inability to do so, throws a kind of ultimate pessimism over the genre. The picaresque novel seems to say that one cannot escape from the world's chaos. If the chances of Fortune do not shatter your withdrawal, your own giddy impulses will.

The general lack of self-control that the picaro experiences is seen by the picaresque novel as typical human behavior. Guzmán cannot control his gluttony at one point (2, 220). Nor can he control his compulsive roguery and tricks: "those Knavish trickes, which I had learned in my youth, were so deeply imprinted in me, that they could not be blotted out" (2, 224).[101] When both these sets of impulses run into the Cardinal's conserves, which Guzmán cannot help but steal, he admits his lack of self-command, but generalizes it: "I knew not what to doe in this case, I was not mine owne man; I had not power over my selfe; and . . . I was one of Eve's sonnes" (2, 246).[102] As he says later, all men are like him: "I imagine with my selfe, that all men are just such as I am; weake, facill, and full of naturall passions; nay, sometimes strange and extravagant humours" (3, 26).[103]

In speaking of the roguery and protean forms of Simplicissimus' chaotic character, we have already touched on his internal instability. Simplicissimus' central instability is religiophilosophic. The hermit, we remember, counseled Simplicissimus to be steadfast in character and avoid the ways of the world,[104] but Simplicissimus utterly fails in his attempts to lead such a stable life.

Even more than Guzmán he continually vacillates between embracing life's chaos and retreating from it into spiritual stability. When, for example, he is about to drown in the Rhine (pp. 258-59), he fervently prays to God and vows "to become a hermit again and do penance for my sins, and be thankful to God's mercy for my hoped-for deliverance till the end of my days" (p. 259).[105] But he is no sooner safe than this resolve is broken. Though such acts of instability and unkept promises are probably familiar to the reader in his own life, Simplicissimus' behavior is the concentrated image of that instability. He wants to leave the corrupt Oliver but cannot because of his internal chaos: "But as I thus plagued and tormented myself and yet could come to no plan . . ." (p. 293).[106] When Simplicissimus decides again to "be a philosopher and to devote myself to a godly life" (p. 333),[107] he is immediately tempted by his "curiosity" to go on the Mummelsee adventure (p. 334). Still later, Simplicissimus leaves the stability and security of his Black Forest farm because of the promise of reward from a colonel (p. 345).[108] Only at the end does his schism resolve itself in favor of retreat, and even then he doubts whether he will, like his father "of blessed memory, persevere therein to the end" (p. 356).[109]

There are other aspects to Simplicissimus' internal instability. He is, for example, extremely imprudent. He is unable to control his vanity, and dresses up in fine clothes though he knows others will be envious (p. 194). When he has money, he is never satisfied, but must have more, and this drive disorganizes his psyche: "From my money I got many foolish plans and strange fancies in my brain . . ." (p. 200).[110] We get the feeling here of a mind in continual ferment. It is a mind that contrasts significantly with the mythical German Hero that "Jupiter" says will bring peace to the earth.[111] Like the picaro, he too is protean: he is capable of being fighter, lawmaker, theologian, and diplomat by turns. But unlike Simplicissimus, he has a steadfast mind focused on bringing "order" and "unity" to the world (pp. 172-77). Simplicissimus, on the other hand, has a mind governed by whim. He has no political or religious loyalties; he is easily persuaded by the Swiss colonel to switch sides in the war (p. 209). In short, he is torn by many of the disrupting passions that he describes in other men at such length (pp. 232-34): evil temper, envy, greed, curiosity, and so forth.

Gil Blas's character, on the other hand, is far from such internal instability. In examining Gil Blas, one discovers indications of instability in some places and of countervailing nonpicaresque stability in others. For example, he shows a picaresque disorganizing vanity (*1*, 78, 80), but also a totally nonpicaresque maturity of response to stress. When a woman innkeeper scorns him because of his poor attire, Gil Blas says, "but this I freely pardoned her" (*1*, 72).[112] Any other picaro would have been driven to rage. In Gil Blas, there is none of the typical picaro's hair-trigger response, highly strung nerves, and subjection of stability to whim. This easy-going maturity reveals part of Le Sage's meaning: it speaks for comic acceptance of the way of the world rather than picaresque rage at the world's disorder.[113]

Stability of character, emotional maturity, and flexibility without anarchy are rather constant in Gil Blas until his first adventures at court. Then he becomes truly unstable. Once again the court, and not the world, emerges as the novel's locus of chaos. At the court, a few words from the Duke of Lerma are enough to make Gil Blas seethe with ambition: " 'Remember that you now belong to the king'—these words of the duke were continually recurring to my mind, and became the seeds of an ambition which increased every instant in my soul" (*3*, 15).[114] With disorganizing ambition comes also disorganizing vanity: "How, after this, could I fail to think myself a person of importance?" (*3*, 24).[115] Sex combines with vanity to make Gil Blas forget his stable self. He makes suit in his own person to Catalina, instead of begging her favors in the name of the Prince of Spain (3, 62). In his actions at court he exhibits a new mixture of motives, getting his benefactor, Don Alphonso, an important post, "less perhaps from friendship than from ostentation" (3, 88).[116]

This new chaos inside him is remarked on by both Gil Blas and his friends: "Avarice and ambition, which possessed me, were entirely changing my disposition. I lost all my cheerfulness; I became abstracted and morose—in fact, a wretched animal" (3, 78).[117] Gil Blas's rejected petitioner Fabricio describes the change from stability to instability thus: "In truth, Gil Blas, you are no longer the same man. Before you were about the court your mind was always at ease, but now you seem perpetually disturbed" (3, 78).[118]

Once Gil Blas is thrown into prison, however, the old stability returns. The reconversion is evidenced particularly in his decision to leave the court when he gets out of prison: "I intended, if ever I should get out of prison, to buy a cottage, and live there like a philosopher" (3, 132).[119] But since the world in *Gil Blas* is not wholly unstable, it is not to be totally abandoned. Though Gil Blas's first impulse is to live an ascetic life, Scipio persuades him to be more easygoing, to retreat from that part of the world which is chaotic but to enjoy the rest of it (3, 135-36). This is an archetypally comic solution in which not all the world is to be abandoned, but rather a new society is to be formed, purged of the unsatisfactory elements in the old one.[120]

Moll Flanders exhibits the internal instability of the traditional picaro, but only in the second half of the book. In the first half, Moll is like a calculating machine, her purpose only to get money and security through marriage. Though this is the contrary of instability, it is such a narrow stability that, when looked at sideways, the character itself seems to disappear entirely, much as Lazarillo's self disappeared at the end of his story.

However, in the second half of the novel, which concerns her thefts rather than her marriages, Moll is as unstable as any picaro. Her mind is torn apart by the fear of capture and her compulsion to rob. The reader gets the impression of a character no longer in control of his actions or emotions. We constantly feel her danger and see her go against her best interests by embracing that danger.

There is also a moral tension besetting Moll's mind. All along she has held conventional middle-class scruples about outright crime, but she yields to "temptations" (p. 192), poverty, avarice, and the "devil" (p. 195) at last. The fall of her character into moral instability is expressed in terms of demonic possession. Almost automatically, she picks up the little bundle a maid-servant leaves out. In this, her first crime, the devil has taken over: "but as the devil carried me out and laid his bait for me"; "the devil, who laid the snare" (p. 195). And a bit later: "the devil put me upon killing the child" (p. 198). When she gets honest work, she is still possessed: "the diligent devil . . . prompted me to go out and take a walk" (p. 203).

After her first robbery, the very streets of London serve as a metaphor for the new chaos of her consciousness. She takes the bundle and in horror she flees, twisting and turning just as her mind has begun to do: "When I went away I had no heart to run, or scarce to mend my pace. I crossed the street indeed, and went down the first turning I came to, and I think it was a street that went through into Fenchurch Street. From thence I crossed and turned through so many ways and turnings that I could never tell which way it was nor where I went" (p. 196). Defoe was apparently so pleased with this device that he used it again two pages later, making it more effective by giving "exact," "realistic" details of London's geography. Moll has thought of being penitent, but "the same wicked impulse" drives her out a second time, completing her corruption into moral instability and compulsive thievery. This is how Defoe at once images her flight, her deranging fear, and her lack of control: "I went through into Bartholomew Close, and then turned round to another passage that goes ino Long Lane, so away into Charterhouse Yard and out into St. John's Street; then, crossing into Smithfield, went down Chick Lane and into Field Lane to Holborn Bridge, when mixing with the crowd of people usually passing there, it was not possible to have been found out" (pp. 198-99). Such specific concrete details are a device of the realistic novel, but they give the impression of solid, ordered reality (that is, *the* reality of the realistic novel) only when the relations between the details are clear and solid. If details are merely listed, they become a picaresque device. Though Defoe's place names may be plotted on a map, in the reading they give the impression not of an ordered map, but of a jumble, a labyrinth in both subject and object, in Moll and in the city, in the individual and in the world.

From this point on, "it was all fear without and dark within" (p. 197). Moll cannot give up robbery, but lives in fear of apprehension: "I could expect no safety, no tranquillity in the possession of what I had gained; [however] a little more, and a little more, was the case still" (p. 212). Such labyrinthine confusion, such lack of self-control, is universal in Moll's world, as Moll's governess feels when she ruminates over the drunken gentleman Moll has robbed: "it so affected her that she was hardly able to forbear tears to think how such a gentleman run a daily risk of being undone every time a glass of wine got into his head" (pp. 234-35).

Though in the end Moll repents, converts, and assumes the mantle of moral stability, she continues to stray outside the law by bribing officials, and to violate her new scruples by wildly lying to everyone. The ending of *Moll Flanders* is ambiguous; yet there is considerable evidence that Moll's conversion does not produce true stability. Besides the bribes and lies, we have Defoe's own words in the Preface: "she lived, it seems, to be very old, but was not so extraordinary a penitent as she was at first; it seems only that indeed she always spoke with abhorrence of her former life, and of every part of it" (p. xxii).

With what has been said of the separate strains in Roderick Random's character, one may expect to find in him a high degree of internal instability. But while there is a good deal of fluctuation in Roderick's character, he does not exhibit the internal instability that characterizes the typical picaresque hero. There is little of the instantaneous in him; he does not make decisions according to whim, but rather according to design and circumstance.[121]

He is also internally stable in his attitude toward the world. Unlike most picaros, he does not alternately embrace and then flee from the world. Roderick decides early that he hates the world but believes that to escape it one must have a lot of money, and money can only be made by entering the world. This approach to the picaresque universe seems simpleminded because it is unworkable. In a typical picaresque universe, such as Smollett's usually is, being upper class does not guarantee security. If the world is crazily chaotic and random, how can any amount of money put one above the world's chances? Smollett creates a picaresque world but puts a partially nonpicaresque character into it. There is nothing wrong, of course, with mixing genres, provided the genres are truly mixed. In *Gil Blas,* for example, the form of the traditional picaresque novel is used as a basis for comedy. One genre exploits another. In *Roderick Random,* however, the relations between the generic elements are not always clear, and the result is a certain incoherence. The genres are not perfectly fused by any shaping spirit—the work lacks, too frequently, an overriding unity of tone.

Roderick at first seems to be unstable like other picaros. He loves Narcissa, for example, but strays when he thinks Miss Sparkles is interested in him into the egotistical fantasy of conquering a rich, handsome lady: "planning triumphs over the malice and contempt of the world" (*3*, 34). But although there are a number of such unstable lapses, they are in fact lapses from the structure of the character.

The fissures within this character also should not be interpreted as instability. Roderick Random is much more a name split into several characters than one being moved by random impulse in different directions. When Smollett's purpose changes, so does the character. Now Roderick must be very good (so as to seem melodramatically oppressed), now he must slip into *picardía* (so as to expose the world's chaos from the point of view of the underworld).

And through the entire novel are certain constant traits that belong to the romance hero. His love for Narcissa is perfect love, described in pure romance language and indicating a constancy of sentiment that is the very opposite of instability: "but now I was elevated by my passion above every other consideration" (*3*, 83). "I . . . discovered . . . the adorable Narcissa! Good Heaven! what were the thrillings of my soul . . . !" (*3*, 81). Another romance trait in Roderick is his bravery. His pride is easily offended, and when it is, as by Crampley, Roderick fights. Roderick's "haughty disposi-tion" (*1*, 8) is still another romance trait. Because this trait is truly a trait and fairly constant, Roderick can talk about his "disposition" as though his character were stable (*1*, 135). For although he is several characters rather than one, each character is firmly established. One must conclude that although there are lapses in character, and the character is split into several pieces, Roderick has so many of the romance hero's flat, stable, and good qualities that calling him internally unstable is inaccurate.

Part Three

Interpretive Devices: Point of
View, Style, and the Ending
of the Picaresque Novel

I

Introduction

N THE SECTIONS ON plot and character, we have seen how the drama of the typical picaresque novel projects a chaotic sense of life. At this point we could consider the many motifs that are used to enhance that sense of disorder. The motif of *law and order* reveals judges, jailers, and policemen as corrupt and venal; the rule of law and order is parodied—just as there is no law behind events, so there is no law in society. Similarly, the motif of the *quack doctor* parodies the order of science; sickness strikes when and where it will and those who are appointed to adjust the disorder of sickness aggravate it instead. The motif of the *corrupt cleric* exposes still another force that should contribute to order but does not. There is the motif of the *madness scene* in which all pretense at personality structure in the picaro cracks. Often, a picaresque novel has several such scenes, each an appropriate reaction to universal disorder. Similarly, almost every picaresque novel has a *vision of paradise* in it. In *The Unfortunate Traveller,* for example, it is a paradisiacal garden that Jack sees in Rome. In *Guzmán de Alfarache,* it is the city of Florence. In *Simplicissimus,* it is Switzerland, the land uninvaded during the Thirty Years War. These scenes and visions contrast with the otherwise universal chaos, pointing up the lack of order in the picaresque world.

Though there is virtually no limit to the number of motifs which might be adduced to reinforce the argument of Parts One and Two, to discuss such motifs would shift our focus away from the form of the picaresque novel directly to its content. Moreover, more urgent and more difficult questions present themselves. If the dramatic aspects of the picaresque novel generate a certain chaotic sense of life, how do the less dramatic, the more interpretive aspects cooperate? What types of narration, what styles, what kinds of endings are typical of picaresque novels?

In answering these questions we run into the obdurate individuality of the work of art. While the dramatic stuff of traditional picaresque novels falls into fairly consistent though somewhat generalized and abstracted patterns, the interpretive stuff is very diverse. One narrator is moral, another is not. One tells the story straightforwardly, another continually interrupts. One believes life can be ordered, another does not. Accordingly, it becomes impossible to induce any ideal picaresque narrator, or, for that matter, any ideal picaresque style or ending.

What one must do, clearly, is to study individual novels and see how a particular narrator, style, or ending fits the implications of plot and character. We may then hope that some more precise notion of what are appropriate points of view, styles, and endings for picaresque novels will emerge, though no single procedure will seem clearly ideal.[1]

Before discussing the diversity of points of view in the picaresque novel, we may remark on one element of unity: the picaresque novel is told, traditionally, from the first person, recollected point of view. The reasons for this procedure are two. The recollected or later point of view, as opposed to the diary/letter first person, gives an air of reliability to the tale.[2] To a certain extent, subjectivity is, or seems to be, excluded from the telling. More importantly, the sustained first person narration forces us to sympathetically identify ourselves (more or less) with the picaro.

This sympathetic identification arising from the first person point of view is basic to the functioning of the picaresque novel. That function has been described as the communication of a sense of life's chaos. But the plot and character of picaresque novels will not seem to their probable readers to have much to do with the way life really is. The settled, educated, middle-class reader who probably read these books in the seventeenth and eighteenth centuries, a type that reads them still, would not have been down and out, would not have engaged in a tremendous variety of occupations, would not have been a professional trickster or criminal, would not have suffered daily rushes of event, would not have been as unstable as the picaro, would not have met almost totally dark experience. Most readers of picaresque novels have led lives that are *literally* far removed from the adventures and characters of the novels.

On the other hand, if the image of life portrayed in the picaresque novel is *literally* far removed from the reader's life, it is not so removed *metaphorically*. We readers are not literally down and out, yet we are daily exposed to something like the struggle for survival: our daily struggle for stability and security. We may not have a variety of occupations, but we play protean roles within a single occupation. We constantly resort to forms of trickery, flattery, and deception to make our way in the world. If we are internally less chaotic than the picaro, it is a difference in degree, not in kind.

The novelist's problem is a difficult one. His novel *must* select and exaggerate certain aspects of life in order to convey its vision in an exciting, heightened, and engrossing way. Yet because of the literal differences between the reader's experience and the picaro's, the novelist risks losing his audience at the outset, so he forestalls the reader's objections to these apparent differences by plunging him into the picaresque world. The novelist puts the reader in full view of only one perspective, the picaro's, and forces him thereby to experience what the picaro experiences. If the reader imaginatively becomes down and out himself, this shocking experience may then reveal meaning for his own life. First, however, he must undergo the experience, and this is encouraged by the first-person point of view.

A good example of how the first-person point of view operates to control our responses is the Fabia episode in *Guzmán*.[3] The plot of the incident is reminiscent of the hoary comic tradition of laughing at amorous attempts to violate the social order. A socially and morally unsuitable suitor for illicit love is defeated by a chaste, virtuous, and clever woman. In such a comic incident, the reader rejoices in the victory of virtue over vice, quick-wittedness over dull pretension. The defeat of the pretentious suitor is laughable and comic, no matter what happens to him, because the story is told from the lady's point of view. The audience identifies itself with intelligence, virtue, and order.

In the *Guzmán* story, the situation is reversed; we identify with the picaro. Instead of serenely experiencing the manipulation and ordering of events from Fabia's point of view, we experience all as disorder from Guzmán's point of view. Each event hits us as a surprise just as it hits the picaro. We plunge with him into the hog sty full of manure and with that into the picaresque world. The boar that rushes out at Guzmán is as much a surprise to us as it is to him.

We share his pain, his rage, and his madness. We participate in the sense of disorder because we participate in the world (as we read the book) only as the picaro does.[4] With Guzmán we undergo those two nights of pain, darkness, and frustration. The inner point of view focused on the picaro is therefore of great importance in making the picaresque novel non-comic. In comedy, the perspective is always above life. In the picaresque novel the perspective is almost always below it.

II

Specific Interpretive Devices

AZARILLO

The character of the narrator in *Lazarillo* is congruous with that of the picaro in the drama. For example, Lazarillo poses as a religious and moral man, but we are supposed to see that he is merely posing and that he is really a cynical opportunist caught in a world without moral order. He portrays himself as religious in his frequent references to God. On the very first page, he prays that his father is "now in Paradise" (p. 27). As teller of the tale, he continually calls on God and refers to his efforts to get enough to eat as "sins" (p. 38). His "sins" (p. 41) again lead him to a bad master, but "God" comes to aid him in stealing from the master. He asks God to forgive him for praying for the funerals of others so he may have enough to eat (p. 43). But then he says that the large number of people who died when he was at the priest's house died "because the Lord, seeing my prolonged and raging death, was pleased to take those people unto Himself in order to give life to me" (p. 44).[5]

Clearly, here is a narrator not with a consistent religious interpretation of life but with a shifting, changing one. He pays lip service to traditional morality but reveals his basic egotism. We see from the handling of the religious pose that Lazarillo the teller is merely a continuation of Lazarillo the chaotic character. The implication of this point of view is that inner chaos is inescapable because outer chaos is. Lazarillo the narrator is an object of irony because he represents himself in a false light. But he is an object of serious

101

contemplation too in that he has not been able to become a stable person. Life forces him to lie even when he tells his own story.

The teller's attitude toward life is purely opportunistic and materialistic, and this too is consistent with his earlier character and with the picaresque world. He addresses the reader at one point, saying: "I am happy, sir, to recount to you these childhood memories to demonstrate how virtuous it is for men to rise from low estate" (pp. 30-31).[6] The blind man is admired as a phenomenon of wisdom and sagacity, because "He had a thousand ways of getting money" (p. 31).[7] Here is anything but a stable ethic.

The end of the novel also demonstrates an appropriate response on the part of the hero to the world he has encountered in the tale. Though the narrator pretends that he has been entirely virtuous, he inadvertently shows that he has sold his wife to the archpriest of a town in return for a secure position. The narrator's attempt to deny that this is the case only reveals him again as a protean liar who continues the character of the picaro in the novel's fictive present.

If there is anything disturbing about the ending of *Lazarillo de Tormes,* it is its finality. The tale is addressed to a certain "Your Worship," to whom, near the end, Lazarillo says: "In this work [town crier] I live today—in the service of God and Your Worship" (p. 82).[8] There is a sense here that by making the enormous sacrifice of personality required of one who would sell his wife, Lazarillo has somehow put a halt to life's irregularity.

The ethical effect is fine and makes the novel a masterpiece of unity. But the novel's unity might have been more inclusive had the ending been consistent with *all* that had gone before. If, as plot and character show, the world is disordered both inside and out, then no single gambit, not even a corrupt one, can still the flux and impose order and stability upon it. The immoral person is still exposed, for example, to the metaphysical chaos represented by such devices as the episodic plot and the Fortune pattern. The ending of *Lazarillo* should be more open. In fact it is.

Closer examination of *Lazarillo* reveals that though the narrator has a job and the picaro-actor has "reached port" in some weird sense, the story is not wholly closed. First, the confessional point of view works to preserve and communicate a sense of the "livingness" and therefore a sense of the final instability of the speaker. He is a living man talking to a man, not merely a voice recording what happened. His tale is addressed to a certain "sir" (p. 27), who has asked him to tell it, and it is being told, as it were, before our eyes. Further enhancing the sense of openness is the fact that the tale reads like a particular piece of rhetoric directed to some unknown but practical end. The "sir" to whom it is addressed has asked Lazarillo to tell his tale fully. But why? Though we are not told why, we cannot help conjecturing the motives for the telling. For example, is Lazarillo in danger of losing his job because he has not denied in print the slander about his wife and the archpriest? We imaginatively perceive the tale not merely as a live utterance but as an utterance in some *real* situation that Lazarillo must yet cope with.

The novel is also open in its style. There is a conversational informality about the telling, a jagged, live quality that suits the vital confusion found in plot and character. The lack of transitions, for example, reflects a mind still disordered. There is a clear attention to what is important but also a felt disorder when Lazarillo tells of his birth in one sentence and begins the next: "Now, when I was eight years old . . ." (p. 27).[9] There is something not quite ordered, not quite static or figured out in a narrator who writes like this and tells his tale in such a halting fashion. Again, such a non-literary, non-logical style is partly inherent in the auto-biographical point of view of many of these novels.

The Unfortunate Traveller

While Lazarillo the narrator pretended to have found a true moral-religious stability only to be revealed as a liar, Jack Wilton the narrator makes little pretense of being different from his picaresque character. As narrator, he rejoices in the tricks of the younger actor. After telling how he tricked a stupid captain, he interrupts the tale to say: "Here let me triumph a while, and ruminate a line or two on the excellence of my wit: but I will not breathe neither till I have disfraughted all my knavery" (p. 217). There is no repentance for roguery and disorder here; rather, joy in recollection. At another point the narrator boasts, "I have done a thousand better jests," and adds, "It is a pity posterity should be deprived of such precious records . . ." (p. 210). In other words, the narrator of *The Unfortunate Traveller* is perfectly consistent with the chaotic picaresque actor in his roguery and general amorality. The narrator has apparently found no inner stability except in the formless impulse of gratuitous roguery. The novel seems to say, by virtue of the narrator's pose, that there is no way out of life's chaos.

But the consistency between the character of the narrator and the character of the picaro is more deeply engraved in the novel's texture than any single focus on roguery could reveal. The consistency is engraved in the narrator's character *qua* narrator. On the very first page he characterizes himself as a drunkard, interrupting the writing of the narrative to have a swig: "There did I (soft, let me drink before I go any further) . . ." (p. 203). He brags of his experience with drink and mentions the "pair of quart pots" before him as he writes (p. 204).

Such comments clearly show that the narrator's character is still disordered. But they do more; they provide a dramatic rationale for the disorder of his *tale*. For the tale is as drunk as the teller—digressive, self-commenting, reader-addressing. It is a tale that refuses to get on with the business of narration. The references to drink cited in the preceding paragraph are examples of this digressive tendency, and dozens of similar digressions could be cited. Because the narrator quite gratuitously refuses to tell his story straight, his tale is chaotic not only in structure (plot and character) but also in texture.[10]

The device seems to me of great significance. In the first place, the digressive manner has a dramatic function, further characterizing the narrator as unchanged from himself as the picaro. In the second place, on the level of style the gratuitous interruptions of the narrative are a development of the jagged open style of *Lazarillo*. In their violation of narrative convention, the lack of transitions in Lazarillo's tale served as a stylistic metaphor for the world's chaos. The refusal of the narrator in *The Unfortunate Traveller* to write a coherent narrative is even more shocking. The reader, used to the usual conventions of fiction, expects the narrator to get on with his tale, but the narrator instead takes a swig from the bottle on his desk. It is an amusing device, but unsettling, contributing greatly to the general emotional effect of the novel. Jack rejoices in his ability to digress: "Wherein let me dilate a little more gravely than the nature of this history requires . . ." (p. 225). He then proceeds to do so, but we wonder by what right. We are made uneasy by Jack's capriciousness, by his insults, and by his insolent commands. Needing a transition to describe the passage of several months, he orders the reader to supply it: "sleep an hour or two, and dream" (p. 218).

All this narrative peculiarity serves also to demonstrate the attitude of the narrator toward reality in the novel: he cannot try to describe it in a serious and continuous way. It is as though life were so ugly and horrible in its chaos that the only thing to do is avoid looking at it. It is as though even the tale were trivial, any tale trivial, and the only things to do are to be witty and get drunk. *The*

Unfortunate Traveller finds the world full of violence and horror, but the attitude of the narrator toward this violence and horror is expressed by nonchalance and witty joking. He seems to say the world is so horrible it is funny: "The executioner needed no exhortation hereunto, for of his own nature was he hackster good enough: old excellent he was at a bone-ache. At the first chop with his wood-knife would he fish for a man's heart, and fetch it out as easily as a plum from the bottom of a porridge pot. He would crack necks as fast as a cook cracks eggs . . ." (p. 307). This is the voice of a man to whom nothing is serious, everything a subject for wit and fun. In modern parlance, such an attitude is "sick." *The Unfortunate Traveller* is full of sick jokes, full of attempts to make the horrible funny. Jack the narrator keeps reality at a distance with his wit, stylistic brilliance, and drink, because reality is simply too horrible to contemplate seriously.

As for the ending, it is open in the same sense as that of *Lazarillo*. The intense characterization of the narrator and his very personal narrative technique all give the impression of life continuing beyond the borders of the story proper. Moreover, the novel is open in still another way. Though Jack at the end says he was "incited" to a "straight life" and then returned to the king of England's camp, this is not the end of his tale, but merely a pause in it. He promises to go on with the story if he has pleased any: "All the conclusive epilogue I will make is this: that if herein I have pleased any, it shall animate me to more pains of this kind. Otherwise I will swear upon an English chronicle never to be outlandish chronicler more while I live. Farewell as many as wish me well" (pp. 307-8). Strictly speaking, this is no ending. The world of the novel will continue if the reader wishes it. Jack has not, he implies here, escaped the picaresque world, because such a world is clearly inescapable. All he has done in concluding the tale is to stop at a convenient place.

Guzmán de Alfarache

As a narrator, Guzmán differs from Jack Wilton in posing throughout as a serious moral character. He would have us believe that he has reformed. Such a pose would be so inconsistent with the chaotic world and the chaotic picaro that we would rush to object to it if the interesting narrative manner did not at the same time indicate a continuing chaos in the mind of the narrator.

Guzmán, like Jack, is an unorthodox narrator with a shocking lack of self-control. The book begins with an elaborate delaying tactic that seems to anticipate *Tristram Shandy*. Like other picaresque narrators, Guzmán starts by trying to tell his own story, but he only gets to that in the third chapter. He decides early that he must discuss his parents first, in order to be logical. But the promised story of his parents is itself delayed by a complex apology for slandering his parents (*1*, 38-39). This is immediately followed by a digression on how plain truth is better than embellishment, which, in turn, is followed by still another digression on the effects of detractors (*1*, 43-44). Finally, only after these six pages, we get to his parents' story, although not yet to his. Even after we have read *Tristram Shandy*, the effect of digression piled upon digression is unsettling, and Guzmán, like Jack, tells the reader to expect to be upset by the mad narrative manner: "I know not what excuse to make thee, but to tell thee, that I doe as Carriers doe, that drive their beasts of burthen before them, who rush the man that meetes them against the wall, or throwes him to the ground, and then say, I cry you mercy, Sir" (*1*, 104-5).[11]

Like Jack Wilton the narrator, Guzmán seems unable to control his narrative. When he has been speaking, at one point, of his first experiences on the road, he mentions the famine in Seville and goes off on a discussion of the corruption of Regidors and how this leads to famine. He even tells an anecdote to illustrate the point. Thus, both comment and interpolated tale break up the narrative line. He makes an effort to return to the main story: "Now let us returne againe into our old way, from which we have digrest," but is immediately carried away to discuss the corruption of "Purveyors and Commissaries" (*1*, 102).[12] He realizes, in the beginning of the next paragraph, "This likewise is somewhat out of the way . . . I treat . . . of mine owne life, and therefore will not meddle with other mens . . ." (*1*, 103).[13] He at last admits he doesn't know if he will be able to control himself, comparing himself to a man on an unruly horse: "For there is no man that is Master of himselfe, when he is on horsebacke" (*1*, 103).[14] The narrator claims to be out of control, to be unable to keep his narrative on the path. Such a narrator corresponds nicely to the picaresque world and to his earlier character as picaro.

But if this narrative technique shocks us and is congruous with the narrator's earlier character, it also differs basically from that of *The Unfortunate Traveller*. Jack *refuses* to control his narration in a chaotic world. He is madcap with a will. Guzmán is *unable* to control his narration because he has too much to say. In his digressions, he is almost desperately trying to make sense out of his chaotic

106

experience, and that is why he cannot control himself. His book is, to some extent, what Wallace Stevens called "the poem of the mind in the act of finding what will suffice." [15] That is to say, Guzmán's narrative eccentricities, however chaotic and shocking, are the mark of a most serious purpose, while Jack's eccentricities indicate exactly the opposite. Yet we must admit that the tension between the teller's trying to tell the story and his trying to interpret it in moral and philosophic statements constantly makes *us* feel an almost painful sense of strain. Jack may be nihilistic, Guzmán not, but Guzmán is so desperate to make sense out of things that he forgets his narrative purpose, and this desperation and confusion help project the picaresque sense of disorder.

The attempt to make sense of his world is a patent failure, for so much of what Guzmán says is contradictory in implication: some of the digressions describe the disordered world of the book and suggest appropriate attitudes toward it, others do not. In relating his parable of discontent, Guzmán seems to sum up very well the chaotic drama of the picaresque novel: "Man's life is a warre-fare upon earth, there is no certainty therein; no settled assurance, no estate that is permanent; no pleasure that is perfect; no content that is true; but all is counterfeit and vaine" (*1,* 147). [16] Such a *vanitas* feeling can easily arise out of the experience of the character in the picaresque world. That world is disordered; there is no help for it, no way of controlling it. Such would also be the implications of the various statements Guzmán makes on the theme of Fortune. [17] But at other times, we meet with optimistic statements from the narrator which seem to say that a moral person who follows appropriate religious practices will lead an ordered life and will be safe from the miseries of Fortune and universal discontent.

Wouldst thou live in health? wouldst thou bee cheerefull and merry? wouldst thou continue free from those disturbances, which might give thee cause to lament? wouldst thou abound in riches? and leade a contented life without melancholly? Take then this rule of me; Make thy dayly account with God, confesse thy selfe unto him every day, as if that very day thou wert to dye.

Let Justice be observed by thee in that manner, as it is defined and set down unto thee, giving to every man that which is his due: Eat of the sweat of thine owne browes, and not of the labours of other men; and to this end, store thou up such riches, as are well and truely gotten; so shalt thou live contentedly, so

107

shalt thou be happy, and every thing shall prosper and thrive with thee, and all shall goe well with thee and thine [*1,* 268-69].[18]

Sometimes such contradictory comments occur even closer together. Having described some of his own cheating adventures at a cook's house, Guzmán digresses on the vanity of keeping a magnificent house, how much trouble it takes, how much men are liable to be cheated by their servants, how this is often their own fault for paying the servants so little (*2,* 37-43). Guzmán seems to be saying here that the practice of simple moral and prudential measures—serious attention to one's estate and giving servants a living wage—will bring order into this sector of human activity. In such digressions as this one, and there are many, Guzmán seems to have found a way out of the flux. The book then seems a mere cautionary tale.

But when we turn the page, we find a darker vision, directly contradicting this one and more consonant with what the dramatic action of the book reveals. After all this talk of what servants and masters should be, Guzmán finds servants' corruption to be universal. That is why he succumbed to it, it "beeing a generall disease" (*2,* 44).[19] The moral recommendations for ordering the world seem belied by this universal corruption. They seem quixotic—an attempt to remove a cancer in the cells with an ice pack. Such again is the effect of Guzmán's repeated preachments about the necessity of a steady job: "For, hee that knowes not how to live by the sweat of his browes, must quickly fall into poverty, as you shall see in the sequell of this Story" (*2,* 78).[20] We are shocked by such naiveté. In the action and in his commentary the narrator has revealed to us a world torn apart by shifts of fortune, and now he tells us to seek steady employment.

Such apparent contradictions seem irreconcilable. Too much of Alemán's energy is spent in constructing such rather simpleminded cautionary recommendations for them to have been meant ironically. The fact that Guzmán digresses continually from his narrative is consistent with the picaresque vision projected by plot and character. It is a tense, desperate drama itself that appropriately fragments the narrative line of a tale of chaos. But the *content* of those digressions is not always appropriate to the drama of the novel. We feel that Alemán has failed in some of them (they form a substantial part of the book) to do intellectual justice to the dark reach of his imaginative vision. There have been various attempts to explain this, the most successful of which may be del Monte's. He sees Alemán as a *"uomo barocco,"* consciously committed to Counter-Reformation religious moralizing—in short, to a belief in the efficacy of good works. On the other hand, his personal experience was darker and more chaotic than this faith could account for and reached in the direction of a more otherworldly philosophy.[21] Whatever the explanation, the contradiction is there. It is a contradiction not merely between narrative and commentary but between parts of the commentary itself.

Yet some of the commentary is of great importance in heightening and bringing to our full consciousness the dark significance of the action. This function should not be slighted even though we recognize that it is not consistently performed. Some of these comments have already been cited as epigraphs to some of the previous parts of this book, but another example may be cited here to show how the commentary functions in enhancing the meaning of plot and character.

At one point, Guzmán calls attention to the general deceitfulness of things: "This contagious infirmitie is so generall, that not onely men, but Beasts and Birds doe likewise therein suffer with them. . . . Stones, though they bee but stones, and without sence, trouble our sence, with their counterfet splendour, and lye, in that they seeme to be that they are not. Time, occasions, and our sences deceive us; and above all, our best and most considerate thoughts" (3, 68).[22] In such a passage as this, the attention of the narrator soars to a higher level than in his moral or cautionary comments. Such philosophic flights give the novel a scope and universality that other picaresque novels, with more intellectually limited narrators, do not have. Such comments help shift the reader's attention from the particular event to the contemplation of all the novel's events, forcing him to universalize the drama of the novel. The reader is forced to scrutinize the whole narrative for its total meaning, to see the picaresque world as a whole and to see his own world in relation to it.

The ending is less felicitous. It seems to show Guzmán having made his peace with the world. He betrays his fellow galley slaves, becomes religious in some real sense, and in general seems to have reached both inner and outer stability. Such an ending fully prepares us for the appearance of the moral narrator we have been listening to all along. It does not, however, agree with the chaos that still seems to trouble that narrator or with the picture of the world that the book's dramatic action gives. Del Monte has registered his dissatisfaction with the book's ending in these terms: "The only conclusion to an itinerary like that of Guzmán would have been antisocial asceticism, not a conversion to the religious norm and an adherence to social practice."[23] But a more open ending in which Guzmán found no stability, whether this-worldly or otherworldly, would be still more appropriate.

It must be admitted that we are given some degree of openness at the end of *Guzmán*. Guzmán refers to a continuation of his story that Alemán had already said was written: "I have given thee a large account of my mis-fortunes. . . . What it was hereafter, thou shalt see in my third and last Part, if God shall give me life . . ." (*4, 353*).[24] This "Third Part" never appeared, so the novel remains open in a historical, if not in a literary, sense. Furthermore, in putting an end to what he has written, Guzmán says he was set "at liberty," not that he was put in a stable position after leaving the galleys.[25] In short, the ending of Alemán's novel remains partially ambiguous in its interpretive implications, just as Guzmán's commentary does. In one way, the ending is open, implying no end to the chaos; in another way, it is closed, implying that prudence, clean living, religion, and social conformity can yield stability even in a picaresque world.

The latter is also, unfortunately, the implication of Alemán's own description of Guzmán's career prefixed to the first volume. He speaks as though Guzmán's career could have been stable and secure if only he had had more good sense and good morals. Alemán talks about Guzmán's "slender consideration," how he was "blinded with . . . false pleasures," "the time which he idly mis-spent," "the calamities, and extreme povertie, whereunto he grew, and the inconsiderate courses which he ran into, because he would not take up himselfe in time" (*1, 20*).[26] Clearly, Alemán's comments here narrow the range of the book's philosophic implications from the metaphysical vision of inner and outer chaos to the narrowly ethical and cautionary. Again, we must admit to finding an occasional confusion of purpose in *Guzmán*. Put another way, the picaresque novel, so often seen as a creature of its time, may have been ahead of its time. Perhaps only in the atheistic climate of the twentieth century, devoid of promises of security in this world or another, may the picaresque novel become what it really is.

El Buscón

The attitude of the narrator in *El Buscón* differs completely from that of the narrator of *Guzmán*. Where Guzmán pretends to moral and religious stability, Pablos barely hints at such an end to chaos. More importantly, where Guzmán the narrator impresses us everywhere with his seriousness of concern toward his narrative, Pablos the narrator, much like the narrator of *The Unfortunate Traveller,* treats his picaresque world as an object fit only for wit. Like Jack Wilton the narrator, he is an extension of the chaotic picaro. At the end, to be sure, he makes a moralistic reflection to the effect that an ordered man will be able to lead an ordered existence: "For a man may change his lifelong habitat, but it will do him no earthly good unless he likewise changes his lifelong habits" (p. 233).[27] The persona of the narrator, however, belies any such change of habits.

The style of the narrator in *El Buscón* reveals his view that life must be treated as a joke. While he is relating the chaotic drama, he continually turns away from it to the world of pure wit and literary artifice. The English translation which has been cited gives some notion, however lame, of this practice. The play on the words "habitat" and "habits," cited at the end of the last paragraph, does not appear in the Spanish, but is typical of the novel's verbal wit elsewhere. Nothing is sacred, nothing is so objectionable that an outright complaint against it is in order. Buscón the narrator makes fun of life's chaos and absurdities, but he accepts the chaos, as the picaro-actor did when he became a picaro.

For example, after relating how his half-brother was whipped to death for stealing, Buscón makes no moral reflection, as Guzmán would, no general reflection of any sort. Instead, he plays on words! "That dear angel died of a whipping in jail. My father took it very hard, for the little fellow was so good that he could steal your heart away" (p. 86).[28] The effect is grotesque in the extreme. There is here a kind of insane sick-joke humor resembling that of the narrator of *The Unfortunate Traveller.* The comparison with Bosch that Castro makes of certain gestures and figures works well for the relationship of the narrator to his narration.[29] The effect, however, is no less arresting and shocking than the combination of Guzmán's seriousness of purpose as narrator and his madness of narrative technique. The narrator's stance is crazy but appropriate for a person who has seen a deranged world and who himself recounts how he was deranged by it.

Now we may wonder if the author of the novel has the same attitude toward the picaresque chaos as the narrator does. This is not a question that can be easily answered. The joking, bantering style of Quevedo in his "Al Lector" [30] does not differ from Pablos', but is it Quevedo who speaks there? It is easy, sometimes, to think the author of a book is ironic toward his narrator when he is not. Wayne Booth cites an example of this apropos of Henry Miller.[31]

But whether we can be sure of the author's attitude or not,

whether Quevedo is urging us to share Pablos' attitude toward life's chaos or not, we can at least say what it is we are given. We are given a picaresque world and the tale of how one man experienced it. We see that his experience of it, his view of it as narrator, his point of view, is *dramatically* congruous with that world. It is an insane reaction, but then the world is insane. If the world is insane, it may be best to joke about it, to bury it under a barrage of verbal wit. To try to make sense of chaos (as Guzmán's unfortunate example showed, in spite of itself) may be just too hopeless. Pablos' view of life is morally and metaphysically pessimistic. He seems to say, in his mad joking about chaos, that no order is possible. Whether this was Quevedo's attitude or not, we cannot know for certain. We are only given Pablos-the-narrator's attitude, which, dramatically, as part of the novel's total vision of inner and outer chaos, is congruous and effective.

There is, however, a similarity, albeit an oblique one, between *Guzmán* and *El Buscón,* when we consider the matter of narrative technique alone, without reference to the narrator. We saw that Guzmán's constant digressions from the narrative broke the narrative line and gave the book something of the same jagged rhythm produced by the abruptness of *Lazarillo* and the willful self-editing of *The Unfortunate Traveller*. A similar rhythm is created in *El Buscón* by the interplay between the narrative (a dramatic continuous action) and the verbal surface. The verbal play constantly interrupts our attention to the narrative as the commentary interrupted it in *Guzmán*. We are constantly torn from the story to consider, ponder, and admire the intense activity of the verbal level. Our attention is constantly alternating between style and action in a way that gives birth to an instantaneous and irregular rhythm in reading the book. This is very different from the self-effacing style of the realistic novel, and most effective for the total purposes of the picaresque. This jagged reading rhythm suggests a correspondence with the jagged episodic plot, its rush of events, the internal chaos of character, and the other dramatic aspects of the picaresque novel.

It is possible to write a picaresque novel in a rather more orthodox style. *Moll Flanders* is more orthodox. But the great stylistic and narrative unorthodoxy of *The Unfortunate Traveller, Guzmán,* and *El Buscón* gives these books a rough, irregular beat that accounts for much of their power. Since a certain amount of this stylistic unorthodoxy is useful in the traditional picaresque novel, it might be included as part of the definition of the genre. Such unorthodoxy seems to characterize many of the modern novels that one is inclined to classify as picaresque. Céline writes in a "crackling" manner, as Alfred Kazin has put it. Nelson Algren's *Walk on the Wild Side* has a Dos Passos roving point of view and mixes many different styles. In Donleavy's *The Ginger Man,* the point of view moves in and out daringly, close up for a peek into Dangerfield's psyche and far out for an overview. The same book even breaks up the smooth prose narrative surface with incidental snatches of verse. The very rhythm of the narration in all these books enforces the vision of an instantaneous and disordered world. Something of this quality is always projected by the style of the picaresque novel because of the first-person point of view. Even *Moll Flanders* partakes of the spoken, the conversational, the instantaneous, and the incomplete. But this basic effect may be properly heightened by some of the devices discovered in *The Unfortunate Traveller, Guzmán,* and *El Buscón.*

The ending of *El Buscón* seems fully congruous with the book's disordered plot, character, and narrator. In the first place, like *Guzmán,* the novel is unfinished, the first edition promising further recitals of Pablos' misfortunes "in the second part" (p. 233). No second part ever appeared. The novel is open at the end in another way, for Pablos implies that the plot of the book goes on forever and that the character never changes his disordered state: "But it turned out worse than ever for me. . . . For a man may change his lifelong habitat, but it will do him no earthly good unless he likewise changes his lifelong habits" (p. 233).[32] The end of this sentence is full of pious morality, but gives us no reason to believe that Pablos did in fact change in character or in *estado*. There is reason even to doubt the moral proposition (possibly put in for the benefit of the Inquisition), since this sentiment is practically the only one of its kind in the book. The world Quevedo has described in the novel would have been chaotic whether Pablos' character changed or not. Had he changed, the change would only have been temporary, since the world would have deranged him again. So the novel remains definitely open, leaving Pablos sailing for the Spanish colonies in America and for a life worse than the already chaotic one he had chosen.

Simplicissimus

Simplicissimus differs from the novels treated so far in that the point of view of the narrator toward his experience is not revealed by lengthy comments as in *Guzmán* nor by continual wit as in *The*

Unfortunate Traveller and *El Buscón*. There is considerable vitality in the telling, and also continual world-weariness, as in such a comment as this: "So I must to horse, and must learn how a single unlucky hour can rob one of all welfare and so separate him from all luck and happiness that all his life he must bear the consequences" (p. 109).[33] Simplicissimus introduces the episode of how he was separated from his wife with another comment that seems to condemn the world: "Things do happen in different fashions. To one man ill luck cometh by degrees and slowly: another it doth fall upon in a heap" (p. 230).[34] The narrator also continually calls attention to how the vagaries of Fortune have buffeted him about. Such world-condemning commentary is a valuable device, enchancing the meaning of the drama just as in *Guzmán*. But at other times, Simplicissimus' is a less searching religious persona. He sometimes sees God ordering things in this world. Sometimes the narrator seems to say that if one is good and pious, life will be good, and if one is bad, life will be bad: "yet had I not such decency and piety as to thank God for bringing me out of such darkness and ignorance, and into greater knowledge and understanding. And how then could I expect that the good fortune which daily rained upon me should endure?" (p. 231).[35] In other words, Simplicissimus the narrator, like Guzmán, takes two diverse attitudes toward the world: (1) the world is fundamentally evil and disordered and should be abandoned; and (2) God orders the world, rewarding the good and punishing the wicked. The first attitude is perfectly consonant with the picture of the world presented in the drama; the second is contrary to it and contradictory of the first attitude.

Some of the most telling commentary in *Simplicissimus* is made not by the narrator but by characters in the story. The narrator's setting them down without comment of his own gives us a sense of his assent to these views. Such, for example, is the implication when the narrator recalls Simplicissimus' first reactions to the world at the fortress of Hanau. The very chapter heading of Book I, Chapter xxiv, gives us the point of view of Simplicissimus the actor toward the world: "How Simplicissimus blamed the world and saw many idols therein."[36] The narrator then records Simplicissimus' reflections thus: "In place of the straightforward dealing which every true Christian should have, I found mere hypocrisy; and besides, such numberless follies among all dwellers in the world that I must needs doubt whether I saw before me Christians or not" (p. 52).[37]

Commentary of this kind, whether within the story or coming directly from the narrator, acts vitally to express the chaos in the

114

world and (when it is turned on him) in Simplicissimus' own character. But such commentary becomes intermittent in the re-counting of Simplicissimus' adventures as the Huntsman of Soest and in other parts of the novel. That is, the serious philosophic condemnation of men and the world that gives the novel much of its character lapses occasionally, and we get a recital of adventures that seem almost purely comic. For example, Chapter xxxi of Book II, "How the devil stole the parson's bacon and how the huntsman caught himself," is almost a pure *divertissement,* which Simplicissi-mus labels as merely "amusing to be heard." [38] These are certainly flaws in the book and inconsistent with the overriding world-condemning point of view.[39]

Simplicissimus' major importance as a narrator is not in his commentary or in any specific philosophic pose. The most signifi-cant thing about him is that he is vivid, changing, alive before our eyes. Even the possible contradictions among his comments may give us the sense of a character constantly changing in accord with a narrative and a narrated world that is not fixed or ordered. As in the other picaresque novels examined, this effect is obtained by a variety of devices.

There are, first, numerous references to the process of composi-tion. A good example occurs early in the novel: "Although it was not my intention to take the peaceloving reader with these troopers to my dad's house and farm, seeing that matters will go ill therein, yet the course of my history demands that I should leave to kind posterity an account of what manner of cruelties were now and again practised in this our German war . . ." (p. 8).[40] We feel in reading such a reflexive comment the very breath of the narrator on the page he is writing. The break in dramatic illusion gives an irregular rhythm to the book, and the vivid life of the narrator forestalls any effect of fixity and completeness that might undercut the picaresque action of the novel.[41]

Simplicissimus' claim to a real historical existence, in the course of his writing, contributes to the vivid effect. He recounts how he was forced to represent a musketeer when the commissary came to inspect the fortress of Hanau. But he writes as though he had to defend himself against accusations of serving the Swedish Crown on other occasions—accusations that are presumably being made at the time of the narration: "And this is all the service that ever I rendered to the Crown of Sweden in all my life: and the enemies of that Crown can at least not lay more than this to my charge" (p. 81).[42] We have been reading along up to this point, perhaps confident of the fictionality of the narrator, when suddenly he erupts into real existence. He is a real man writing his memoirs, not just a narrator. We are startled; the rhythm of narration is broken up; we are aware of a live and unfinished action.

Simplicissimus' very comments about the action have a similar effect in interrupting the narrative, showing as they do the narrator's struggle for meaning in a disordered world. But the effect of vividness and incompleteness is best achieved in *Simplicissimus* by its sudden rushes of style. A rush of nouns such as the following suddenly breaks through a more usual noun-verb style: "For gluttony and drunkenness, hunger and thirst, wenching and dicing and playing, riot and roaring, murdering and being murdered, slaying and being slain, torturing and being tortured, hunting and being hunted, harrying and being harried . . ." (pp. 33-34).[43] The list goes on still further before we come to a verb. Then the wave subsides, and its rush will be followed by a calm, forward march of the narration until we are given another wave. Like the rush of events, the rush of language is dazzling in its effect on us. More important, it gives to the very texture of the narrative the discontinuous quality that seems appropriate to the novel's drama. It is as though the narrator had been madly caught up in the rush of words.

The ending of *Simplicissimus* also fits the meaning of picaresque character, action, and point of view. The novel, in its first edition, appears to end in some definitive way, but actually only comes to rest. At the end of the five books that constitute the original edition, the hero records that he left "the world again and became a hermit" (p. 356).

Such a response to a chaotic world is a rational one, but, we ask ourselves, is it a possible one? Simplicissimus the narrator himself indicates his own doubt about whether he will succeed as a hermit: "but whether I shall, like my father of blessed memory, persevere therein to the end, I know not. God grant us all His grace that we may all alike obtain from Him what doth concern us most, namely, a happy END" (p. 356).[44] The ending here looks in two directions: forward, at a stable, ordered existence as a hermit; backward, at the difficulty Simplicissimus has previously had in ordering his existence. Simplicissimus has tried before to be a hermit, but failed because the war (the novel's principal symbol of outer chaos) interrupted his retreat. Simplicissimus also tried to "be a philosopher and to devote [himself] to a godly life" (p. 333),[45] but was too unstable to resist going on his Mummelsee adventures. He was converted when frightened by the devil, but later slid back to his old involve-

116

ment in the chaotic world (p. 308). Because the ending of the novel makes us remember the forces, both inner and outer, that make for chaos, it is not as final an ending as it might first appear. One may reasonably desire to put aside the chaos of the world by retreat, and the chaos of one's personality by discipline. Yet *Simplicissimus,* with its profound understanding of the omnipresence and potency of these forces, cannot speak in its ending of any truly final victory over them. Such an ending may be a human possibility, but it is the eternal defeat of such aspirations that the picaresque novel typically implies.

Gil Blas

Just as the drama of *Gil Blas* differs radically from that of other classic picaresque novels, so do the interpretive devices. The narrator's point of view toward the world is detached and ironic. A little humpback is received by the Marchioness de Chaves in Book IV, Chapter viii. She tells Gil Blas to let the humpback come to her in her room as privately as possible. For Gil Blas the character, this is monstrous. The implied immorality of his mistress is bad enough without her succumbing to "depraved taste." But to Gil Blas the narrator, this behavior is part of the corrupt way of the world: some are gulls and some are rogues. One accepts this state of affairs with irony:

> How ill I judged of my mistress! The little humpback dabbled in magic; and as his skill had been extolled to the marchioness, who was very apt to believe such imposters, she held private conferences with him, in which he showed her things in a crystal, taught her to turn a sieve, and revealed for money all the mysteries of the cabala. In other words, and to give that man his true character, he was a rogue who lived at the expense of overcredulous people, and who was said to have levied contributions from several ladies of quality [2, 93].[46]

There is none of the almost frenzied outrage of Guzmán, the world-weariness of Simplicissimus, the mad joking of Wilton or Pablos, or the grim acceptance of Lazarillo. This is a civilized response to the corruptions of civilization. The world is full of good and bad, and one accepts that situation. This is the response of a stable narrator, one much in harmony with himself and with the world.

Just as the character of Gil Blas is submerged in his novel, so is the

117

narrator. Many stories told by others are inserted. The tale of Chapter vii of Book II is told by Diego de la Fuenta, Chapter vii of Book III by Don Pompeyo, Chapter xi of Book I by Donna Mencia, etc. The vital picaresque narrator has been removed in all these instances and replaced by someone else, generally of a much more literary type. Gil Blas the narrator is a pale figure beside the other picaresque narrators we have met, and the shifts to other, still paler narrators in his novel continually keep what is told at arm's length from the reader. There is no danger of his being sympathetically dragged into the action, which remains an object of ironic contemplation for him, as for Gil Blas the narrator.

In still other ways, the vivid, incomplete narration of earlier novels is left behind. There is none of the old verve or instantaneous effect in Gil Blas's style. There are few addresses to the reader, few digressive comments, few references to the process of composition. We get no sense of a real subjectivity disturbed by the world's chaos and telling about it. One might trace all these shifts, together with the shifts in action and characterization, to the neoclassic world in which Le Sage lived. Yet we must admit that the new form and content of *Gil Blas* make it so different from earlier (and later) picaresque novels as to make any definition which would include it too broad to be useful. We would then be where we started, with a definition of the picaresque novel that did not go further than collecting adjectives like "episodic," "roguish," and "realistic," without connecting these observable aspects into an image or model of a genre that is really one genre, unified by form and content.

Moll Flanders

Moll Flanders is somewhat different from the other picaresque novels considered. A number of its interpretive devices seem to contradict the implications of the novel's drama, but on closer inspection this contradiction, with the exception of the ending, is revealed as only apparent. The Preface to the novel, for example, gives a rather simple and non-picaresque view of the book's plot. Written by Moll's ghost-writer, it sees the plot governed not by chaos but by poetic justice. Every wicked action in the book is shown as "first and last rendered unhappy and unfortunate" (p. xx). The reader is also to be edified by viewing the tale as cautionary, learning that there are criminals about and that one should not facilitate their crimes, as Moll's victims do, by being imprudent. The pattern of Fortune which the book's action discovers is swept away by the ghost's unrelenting belief in industry: "no case can be so low, so despicable, or so empty of prospect, but that an unwearied industry will go a great way to deliver us from it, will in time raise the meanest creature to appear again in the world" (p. xxi). In short, the ghost's professed interpretation of Moll's life is that she had herself to blame for her troubles, the world is tough but industry and goodness will be rewarded, and evil will always be punished. This is such a narrowly ethical point of view toward the picaresque chaos and such a naive interpretation of the novel's drama that one is tempted to disbelieve it.

This impression is confirmed upon examination of the ghost's character. Having expressed his apologies for the novel and having noted that "these are fully sufficient to justify any man in recommending it to the world, and much more to justify the publication of it" (p. xxi), he laments not being able to tell two of "the most beautiful parts" of the story, namely, the picaresque histories of Moll's governess and her Lancashire husband. The ghost's morality is unconsciously betrayed by his avid interest in these criminal tales: "The second is the life of her transported husband, a highwayman, who, it seems, lived a twelve years' life of successful villainy upon the road, and even at last came off so well as to be a volunteer transport, not a convict; and in whose life there is an incredible variety" (p. xxi). There is something so "goody-goody" about the ghost's moral pose, and something so obviously delightful for him in tales of criminals for their own sake, that the discerning reader cannot take his view of the story seriously. The ghost is not even aware enough to know his own mind. The Preface serves a double purpose. It gets the book past the objections of the Puritans who formed a large part of Defoe's audience. At the same time, it warns the more sophisticated reader not to take such a naive view of the novel lest he seem as ridiculous as the ghost.

The character of the narrator corresponds to that of the ghost. She is unaware of her self, and her moral pose is just a pose, hiding considerable instability of personality. Though at the end she joins society, she condemns its treatment of the orphans of criminals. We feel her trying not to be hard on society as she relates her early life and compares the good care of such orphans in France with the lack of it in England. Instead of bitterly criticizing the English system, she merely remarks, "But the case was otherwise here" (p. 2). Her brevity gives us the feeling that she is trying not to step out of her stable, moral, prosociety pose. We feel an inner tension. Moll the narrator is trying to be quiet and good but is not quite able to put

119

the blame for everything on herself. Here, once again, is a wavering narrator, full of internal tension and discontinuity.

Moll tries hard to maintain a stable moral pose, but we always perceive the chaos underneath it. In recounting the death of her first husband, she "confesses" that she was not properly affected, had never loved him as she ought, and that he was deserving of all a woman could give. She explains that his brother's being near "was a continual snare to me, and I never was in bed with my husband but I wished myself in the arms of his brother; and though his brother never offered me the least kindness that way after our marriage . . . yet it was impossible for me to do so to him; in short, I committed adultery and incest with him every day in my desires, which, without doubt, was as effectually criminal" (p. 55). Are we to believe, can we believe, that Moll really feels what she says in that last clause? The use of the fancy word, "effectually," suggests she is handling the moral sentiment at arm's length. We feel underneath the moral pose a narrator no more settled than the picaro she was.

The jagged effect of narration is not achieved in *Moll Flanders* by the battery of unusual rhetorical and stylistic tricks of the earlier picaresque novel. It is the informality, the conversational quality of the prose, which helps to give this narrative an instantaneous quality, as though what Moll said on the next page might change everything. Consider, for example, this paragraph:

> Upon serious consideration, for indeed now I began to consider things very seriously, and never till now, I resolved to tell him of it first, and it was not long before I had an opportunity, for the very next day his brother went to London upon some business, and the family being out a-visiting, just as it had happened before, and as indeed was often the case, he came according to his custom, to spend an hour or two with Mrs. Betty [p. 27].

In reading this we feel that the narrator is still with us, alive. The numerous parenthetical clauses break up any smoothness. The piling up of clause on clause by means of the conjunctions "and" and "for" gives a racing quality to the narrative. Moreover, the sense of tension between Moll's vigorous lack of literary style and the dressing up the ghost-writer is felt to have done endows the narrative with a queer individual life. Nothing is fixed or settled.

The conversational style, which gives such an open and fragmented effect to the narrative, has many aspects. There is Moll the narrator who describes a scene (p. 150) and then fills us in on some background details, finally calling us back to the scene with a chatty, "But to return to this question" (p. 151). She manages the narrative before our eyes, rather than letting the story tell itself: "I must now come back to brother Robin . . ." (p. 54). There is Moll the narrator who comes close to our ear to confide: "The truth is . . ." (p. 157). She digresses to lecture us or others: "Would such gentlemen but consider the contemptible thoughts which the very women they are concerned with in such cases as these have of them, it would be a surfeit to them" (p. 234). In these and other ways, the surface of the narrative ripples with life. The effect is more subdued than in Baroque picaresque novels, but still very helpful in producing the total sense of chaos.

The ending of *Moll Flanders*, however, seems incoherent. If Moll's conversion at the end does not indicate any great stabilizing of character, the ending, viewed as a whole, has many elements of stable romance and comic endings and carries with it a general feeling of stability achieved at last. In a sudden emergence of the dance pattern Moll coincidentally meets her Lancashire husband in prison.[47] They resolve to reunite and go to the colonies together. Of course, there is the problem of her brother, the husband in America with whom she had committed incest. He conveniently dies. Moll's mother, another reminder of the chaotic past, is similarly removed, and a new family group forms with the union of Moll, her son by incest, and her highwayman husband. The final union of a new family or new society is a pattern belonging to optimistic comedy. The coincidences (meeting the Lancashire husband again and the convenient deaths of the interfering) are elements of the romance plot. Both union and coincidences bespeak a providential order in the universe that is conspicuously absent in the rest of the book.

The ending of the book is also full of other intimations of stability. There is the atmosphere of religious stability, Moll recording that she gave "thankfulness to the hand of Providence, which had done such wonders for me . . ." (p. 350). This guiding hand has also led to economic stability, Moll and her husband becoming prosperous plantation owners. Before they go to America, the ending of the book is full of the cheery, stable, and cozy atmosphere of a Dickens parlor: "In a word, we went all on shore . . . and supped together in Gravesend, where we were very merry . . ." (p. 331). When the couple reach America, the same special atmosphere of solid good feeling and good living is recalled again: "we had a bowl of punch there made of rum, etc., and were very merry" (p. 333). What has happened to produce this continued stability that clashes with the meaning of the book's drama? Moll's character after her conversion has been left open, as we have seen; why not the ending as a whole? Has Defoe's grasp of his materials weakened?

If the ending differs radically in its implications from those of the plot, character, narrator's character, narrative manner, etc., it is probably because strong literary and religious traditions were operating on Defoe as he wrote. As a Puritan, Defoe probably felt the necessity of making Moll's end edifying. She should reform and grow rich; or as the title page puts it, "grew Rich, liv'd Honest, and died a Penitent." As a writer in a neoclassic age, Defoe probably felt his novel should have some conclusive ending.

Even the Baroque picaresque novelists did not end their books in a relentlessly open manner. Except for *El Buscón,* all, in greater or lesser degree, *appear* closed. Defoe must have felt the pressure of the tradition of the closed ending even more strongly. Furthermore, the "happy ending" has always been the desire of all popular audiences and the moral ending that of all Puritan audiences. In writing the ending, Defoe's imagination was probably caught between his personal picaresque experience and the well-learned lessons of religion and criticism.

One might object here that Defoe wants us to view the ending ironically, just as we have viewed the ghost's Preface and Moll's narrative persona ironically. We saw that they were not what they appeared; let us try to consider the ending as merely an appearance for the benefit of Defoe's reading public. But one cannot view the ending this way. So much imaginative energy is expanded on the closing of it, so many tricks of style, atmosphere, and plot, that we feel we are supposed to believe in its implications. We feel we are supposed to believe that the world is ordered in a moral way and that stability of many kinds is possible. Yet, we simply cannot believe these implications of the ending in the light of what has gone before. Tradition would seem to have undermined the novel's ironic balance.[48]

Roderick Random

The Preface of *Roderick Random* prepares us for the picaresque parts of the novel that are to follow and also distracts us from them by calling our attention to some of the book's other interests. Unlike the ghost in *Moll Flanders,* Smollett makes no claims to represent a world ordered by poetic justice, nor does he take a narrowly moral interpretation, blaming Roderick's trouble in the chaotic world on him alone. He says his tale will expose "the knavery and foibles of life" (*1*, xli). He refers to the "sordid and vicious disposition of the world" (*1*, xli) and the "selfishness, envy, malice, and base indifference of mankind" (*1*, xlii). All these comments serve as a kind of prelude to the ethical chaos that is part of the vision of most picaresque novels. But they are all merely ethical comments. They leave out of account any of the metaphysical resonance of such things as the Fortune pattern. They only focus on one aspect of the chaos that exists in this book.

The Preface also fails as a prelude to the book's disorder in its frank and critical discussion of the novel's composition. Almost being his own literary critic, Smollett puts the book at a distance to explain his technique in writing it. There is a short history of the romance, and references to the practice of Cervantes and Le Sage. Such learning and critical distance seem out of place in a preface to a picaresque novel. Such a preface, like Quevedo's note to the reader in *El Buscón,* should probably immerse the reader in the picaresque chaos rather than cause him to consider the novel objectively as a work of art.

The Preface also turns our attention from the novel's picaresque elements to its comic ones. Smollett refers to the "entertainment" the reader will find "in viewing those parts of life, where the humours and passions are undisguised by affectation, ceremony, or education; and the whimsical peculiarities of disposition appear as nature has planted them" (*1*, xlii). Our attention here is keyed for comic incidents, and while there are some in *Roderick Random,* they really sit no better with the picaresque parts of the novel than "entertainment" and "whimsical peculiarities" sit with "the sordid and vicious disposition of the world."

The persona of the narrator in *Roderick Random* is not wholly appropriate to the picaresque world depicted in the book. Roderick's style as narrator indicates his ironic detachment from the action. Here is the first sentence of the novel: "I was born in the northern part of this united kingdom, in the house of my grandfather; a gentleman of considerable fortune and influence, who had, on many occasions, signalised himself in behalf of his country; and was remarkable for his abilities in the law, which he exercised with great success, in the station of a judge, particularly against beggars, for whom he had a singular aversion" (*1*, 1). The tone here is biting, but dry. We feel that the narrator is removed from his world and able to contemplate it from an ironic distance in perfect security.

The style further indicates the narrator's detachment by employing the heavily abstract euphemistic language of the eighteenth-century literary gentleman, even when Roderick describes his earlier discomforts and agony: "As I was now capable of reflection, I began to consider my precarious situation; that I was utterly abandoned by those whose duty it was to protect me; and that my sole dependence . . ." (*1*, 26). Sometimes the narrator drops his literary pose and speaks more straightforwardly about the chaotic world, but even then the style is that of a literary man in complete mental command of his previous experience: "We travelled half a mile without exchanging one word; my thoughts being engrossed by the knavery of the world, to which I must be daily exposed; and the contemplation of my finances, which began sensibly to diminish" (*1*, 63).

This detached style, whether ironic or not, is not helpful in giving us the feel of the book's picaresque parts. There is nothing jagged or wild, strained or tense about it. When Roderick is falsely accused of a crime by a bawd and taken before a judge who ignorantly mistakes his friend Jackson for a well-known criminal, there is an instructive difference between the rough conversation of the judge and Roderick's urbane measured prose: " 'Who are you, sir? Do you give me the lie? Take notice, gentlemen, here's a fellow who affronts me upon the bench; but I'll lay you fast, sirrah, I will; for notwithstanding your laced jacket, I believe you are a notorious felon' " (*1*, 124). Contrast the violent rhythms of speech in the picaresque world of London low-life and false justice with the narrator's measured prose: "My friend was so much abashed at this menace, which was thundered out with great vociferation, that he changed colour, and remained speechless." The jagged rhythms of direct speech fit the picaresque world and express it, but the narrator's literary style removes us from that world.

The style gives rise to an image of the narrator which is also non-picaresque in its implications. Roderick the narrator is an eighteenth-century man trained in the literary conventions of English neoclassicism. He is the humane man of letters who transcends in his style the chaos of his earlier character and of the world in general. The implication is that the world is chaotic and people may be so too, but that there are alternatives to this disorganization. The contemplative pose of the narrator represents such an alternative. Though the narrator's detachment, his calm of mind, throws the world's chaos into relief in *Roderick Random,* though it shows how different the world is from the norms and expectations of civilized man, it also seems to say that the world can be overcome to the extent that we can finally contemplate it and calmly despise it.

On occasion, however, the style seems to move away from neoclassic harmony to truly project the disorder the book discovers in its world. Roderick is being assaulted by a press gang:

> Not being of a humour to relish such treatment, I disengaged myself of the assailant, and with one blow of my cudgel, laid him motionless on the ground; and perceiving myself surrounded in a trice, by ten or a dozen more, exerted myself with such dexterity and success, that some of my opponents were fain to attack me with drawn cutlasses; and, after an obstinate engagement, in which I received a large wound on my head, and another on my left cheek, I was disarmed, taken prisoner, and carried on board a pressing tender, where, after being pinioned like a malefactor, I was thrust down into the hold among a parcel of miserable wretches, the sight of whom wellnigh distracted me [2, 31].

One notices how the measured pace of the neoclassic prose is broken up, after "cutlasses," by numerous parenthetical clauses. The word "cutlasses" is followed by an "and," but the clause being connected here must wait a line and a half to be completed with "I was disarmed." The clause "where I was thrust down" is broken up by the parenthetical "after being pinioned like a malefactor." And the sentence has an almost breathless run-on effect after "I was thrust down into the hold." The "among a parcel of miserable wretches, the sight of whom well-nigh distracted me," seems to fly off the proper end of the sentence, breaking the symmetrical mold of neoclassic style. Such an excited style as that of the latter part of the sentence seems to express the picaresque rush of events and ugly chaos of navy life much better than the style of much of the book. (Cf. 2, 45 and 62, for other examples of picaresque style in the novel.)

The prevailing style and the narrator's pose that goes with it are also sometimes shattered by the eruption of a romantic or melodramatic style. This style soars clearly, as when the narrator relates how he was reunited with Narcissa: "You whose souls are susceptible of the most delicate impressions, whose tender bosoms have felt the affecting vicissitudes of love, who have suffered an absence of eighteen long months from the dear object of your hope, and found at your return the melting fair, as kind and as constant as your heart could wish, do me justice on this occasion . . ." (3, 201). Here we no longer have the balance of the comic-ironic voice nor the disharmonies of the occasional picaresque style. Here the detached pose is suddenly dropped and the style builds upward in a clear line that is anything but representative of picaresque disorder: "You whose souls . . . whose tender bosoms . . . who have suffered . . . and found. . . ." Finally, reaching a peak, the sentence soars to the heights of emotion: "do me justice. . . ."

To some extent, the narrator's personae and styles reflect the confusion of purpose in the novel that we have seen before. One should stress, however, that the dominant style does not so far remove us from the book's picaresque elements that we cannot recognize them for what they are. Scene after scene of chaos in *Roderick Random* qualifies it to be considered among picaresque novels, even if the style is not the most appropriate one and the book is confused.

While the comic-romance ending of *Roderick Random* does not come as a complete surprise, because of the removed point of view of the narrator and certain constant romance traits in Roderick's character, nevertheless it is so implausible in the light of what has gone before that we are amused by it. The first two volumes of the novel are essentially picaresque. We watch Roderick nearly go mad as a captive at sea and a prisoner on land. We watch parody after parody of justice. We watch the homosexual perversion of London society. We are shown the chaos and corruption existing at every level of the royal navy. We see Roderick whirled about by the wheels of Fortune. We are given, in short, a large look at a world full of chaos.

The ending, however, shows us a world full of the order of the romance. Having been separated from Narcissa by poverty, pirates, and the injustice of Squire Timothy, Roderick suddenly and coincidentally meets her again in Chapter 55. Then, in Chapter 60, Roderick meets a man named Don Rodrigo. Mysterious forces, hitherto unfelt in the novel, are suddenly at work: "I had been struck with a profound veneration for him at his first coming into the room" (*3, 182*). The stranger is, of course, Roderick's long-lost father, now coincidentally recovered, rich, and benevolent. Lest there be any doubt that the picaresque disorder of the earlier parts has been surmounted, Don Rodrigo and Roderick call explicit attention to a religious ordering of events that is wholly new in the novel: " 'Gracious Powers!' cried the stranger, starting up. . . . 'O bounteous Heaven!' exclaimed Don Rodrigo, springing across the table. . . . At length he broke out into, 'Mysterious Providence!' " (*3, 185*).

Until now, religion had been largely absent from the book. A new vision of a just world also suddenly erupts at the end—the good are exalted, the evil punished roundly. Faced with the necessity of an ending, Smollett has supplied one, but its vapid cliché quality makes one feel that even he did not believe in it.

Conclusion and Speculative Postscript

Conclusion and Speculative Postscript

T IS NOW POSSIBLE TO summarize the results of this investigation by constructing a model of the typical picaresque novel which is different from other genres. A picaresque novel is a novel with an episodic plot. The episodic plot, together with the Fortune pattern, the accident motif, and the rush of events pattern, projects a universe in a state of chaos. This universe is different from the worlds implied by patterns of action in romance, comedy, tragedy, and the realistic novel because the plot patterns in these types of fiction are different.

The hero of the picaresque novel differs from characters in other types of fiction. His origins are uncertain. He becomes a rogue in a world full of roguery. His roguery differs from comic roguery in being gratuitous. He cannot love or feel strong emotion; he is incapable of anchoring his personality to some idea or ideal of conduct. His internal chaos is externally reflected in his protean roles. This instability of personality is seen in the picaresque novel as a reflection of the outer chaos discovered by the plot patterns. The picaresque character is not merely a rogue, and his chaos of personality is greater than any purely moral chaos. It reflects a total lack of structure in the world, not merely a lack of ethical or social structure.

The picaresque novel generally limits its point of view to the picaro. It may or may not be autobiographical; the essential thing is that the reader identifies himself with the protagonist and vicariously undergoes the shocks of his chaotic experience. When a reader is shocked and dazed he feels the characteristic emotional effect of the picaresque novel—a temporary disorganization of feeling. The picaresque novel is typically written in an unorthodox irregular style in order to enhance its effect. When the picaro or other narrator comments on experience, the comments elucidate and elaborate the vision of universal disorder projected by the more dramatic aspects of the novel. Since that disorder is universal and continuing, it cannot be escaped except in death. Therefore, the picaresque novel has a more or less open ending.

The picaresque novel, we must conclude, is a genuinely distinct genre. We recognize in it a group of formal devices directed toward projecting a unique sense of life. It is not a "realistic" rendering of historical circumstances nor a sloppy precursor of the realistic novel. It is different in form and content from comedy and the comic novel.

This definition, systematically relating form to content, is precise enough to tell us why critics have been reluctant to classify certain early novels as picaresque, although they may exhibit some picaresque characteristics. As I have shown that *Gil Blas* is not a picaresque novel, so it could be shown that *Don Quixote, Tom Jones, Joseph Andrews, Jonathan Wild,* and *Le Roman comique* are not picaresque. This definition also allows us, by way of speculative postscript, to say a few words about what happens to the picaresque genre after its classic period. I must, however, reserve the right to call such comments speculative because they are not really part of my task here, and the later history of the picaresque certainly deserves a book of its own.

Generally speaking, one can say that the picaresque novel disappears in the latter half of the eighteenth century and in the nineteenth century as well. The reader will no doubt have noticed that in the last three examples, *Moll Flanders, Gil Blas,* and *Roderick Random,* there is a gradual attenuation of the pattern for the picaresque novel established in the seventeenth century. It is difficult to find any important novel later in the eighteenth century, or in the nineteenth, that substantially follows the traditional pattern. Numerous names have been suggested, *Le Rouge et le Noir, Huckleberry Finn, Dead Souls, The Pickwick Papers,* and so forth, but except for partially preserving the episodic pattern and incorporating a certain amount of roguery, these novels do not express a chaotic sense of life in the way that the traditional picaresque novel does. It will be seen by a glance at the titles proposed that the word "picaresque" has been applied to such a variety of novels in the past that it can

132

scarcely mean anything unless we find some valid way to restrict its meaning.

One may speculate at some length about reasons for the disappearance of the picaresque novel in the eighteenth and nineteenth century. From the point of view of literary history there is no doubt that the triumph of the realistic novel drove out most of the other subgenres. The great artists were all working to establish another tradition. It may also be that the gradual triumph of the physical sciences gave men such a strong feeling that the universe was ordered by laws that the picaresque novel could not express their sense of life. Whatever the reason, the picaresque novel seems to disappear between 1750 and 1900, but undergoes a revival in the twentieth century. That revival has reached such proportions now, and the term picaresque has achieved such currency in literary discussions, that one cannot pick up a literary magazine without reading about someone's purportedly "picaresque" novel.

The recent novels sometimes called picaresque are almost without number: one or more of the novels of Céline, Henry Miller, Nelson Algren, Thomas Pynchon, William Burroughs, Ralph Ellison, Jean Genet, Günther Grass, James Donleavy, Saul Bellow, Thomas Mann, and so forth. It may be that all of the books in question conform to the traditional patterns of the picaresque enough to assign them to the genre. I have my doubts. *Felix Krull,* for example, seems to me more comic than picaresque; it celebrates the triumph of imagination over experience more than the submission of the individual personality to chaos. Critics have recently been inclined to call any "jazzy" episodic novel with a roguish hero a picaresque novel; I would be more inclined to make distinctions. There is no doubt that the twentieth century, like the seventeenth, in which the picaresque began, is unusually sensitive to the chaos of experience. The revival of picaresque patterns in recent fiction probably arises from our need to find vehicles to express our own varied senses of disorder. But in many cases, the sense of disorder expressed by recent novelists is not truly picaresque in the traditional sense.

The novels which have philosophical absurdity as their theme, for example, are probably not picaresque. *Catch-22* seems to use some of the traditional picaresque devices, but does not really. When a modern writer wishes to convey a sense of the absurdity of the universe, he is not trying to shock the reader in the same way that picaresque novelists did. A world which is lamentable because it gives the human being no final philosophic answers is, for whatever it may be worth, a much more relaxed world than the picaresque one. In the picaresque world, the chaos is radical; it extends to the very roots of life. In a picaresque novel one has as much chance of being run over by a cart if one steps into the street as not—and the reader is supposed to take such a view of his chances as literally true (at least while he is reading the book). Such a gratuitous incident in an "absurd" novel is always felt as symbolic, not as something to which a reader reacts immediately but as pointing to a lack of sensible ordering in the universe on a level far above that of daily life: "God is blind or malicious, anything can happen." When one reads a picaresque novel, he gradually comes to feel that he may be in physical danger sitting in his armchair—such is the nature of the world the picaresque novel reveals. When one reads an "absurd" novel his anxiety is much less immediate, though it may be even more important.

We could probably use our knowledge of the traditional picaresque novel as a fixed point by which to find our way through much of contemporary fiction. The definition we have arrived at could well serve as a means by which we could distinguish various strains in novels that look alike but really are not. I have suggested here that among recent novels sometimes called picaresque, one is really a comic novel and the other, for want of a better term, is a novel of absurdity. Henry Miller's novels also seem to me comic, and one could go on in this way.

Here, however, it is only proper to examine briefly a contemporary novel that *is* picaresque in the traditional sense, and to suggest why such a classification is valuable for criticism. I have in mind Ralph Ellison's *Invisible Man:* in nearly every respect it conforms to the old patterns. It is episodic in plot and full of accident. Indeed, one can say that the basic emotion the hero experiences is surprise. He is surprised when the speech he is to make at a men's club turns into a riot; he is surprised when an innocent drive in the country results in his expulsion from school; he is surprised when the leadership of the Brotherhood betrays the Negro in the interest of all men's freedom, and so on. Like the traditional picaro, he is surprised at the whirling alternations of good and bad fortune: one day he is a successful college student, the next a bum, and the next a leader of the Brotherhood. He is tormented, like his literary ancestors, by violent rushes of event: the explosion in the paint factory, the lobotomy scene, the final race riot in Harlem are all expressive of a sense of life's chaos similar to what we found in our classic examples.

In his character, the Invisible Man resembles the older picaro too.

As the title indicates, the character is without self or definition. Though he wants to love, all his experience makes it impossible to maintain a stable affection. The alternations of his feelings toward Clifton, or Ras, are examples of this. Like the older picaro, he too is lonely: he is invisible not only in lacking a self but because no one sees him; all of us are invisible to one another, the novel seems to claim. Like the older picaro again, the Invisible Man is protean: he is a laborer in a paint factory, college student, chauffeur, rabble-rouser, political organizer, and anarchist criminal. And finally, like the older picaro, he is a trickster; like him, he is taught by the world to be a rogue; like him, he begins to embrace trickery for its own sake or as a protest against the nature of the world's disorder.

In its interpretive devices, this novel is also remarkably close to the earlier picaresque masterpieces. The style is crackling and varied in the extreme: it mixes poetry and prose, formal English and Negro slang, literary allusion and scientific reference. Take the opening lines: "I am an invisible man. No, I am not a spook like those who haunted Edgar Allan Poe; nor am I one of your Hollywood-movie ectoplasms. I am a man of substance, of flesh and bone, fiber and liquids—and I might even be said to possess a mind." Besides mixing levels of style here, Ellison is also exploiting short sentences, abrupt clauses, and rhythmic repetition to achieve the intense and jagged effect that is typical of the earlier picaresque. As the style is disordered, so is the narrative point of view. This is in keeping with the chaotic world that Ellison discovers. The ending of the book is open, too, the narrator deciding with touching hopefulness to come out of the hole the world has made him fall into. What will he find but more of the chaos he has already discovered?

Apart from a certain inherent interest there may be in associating a modern Negro novel with the traditional picaresque, there may also be a critical, or explicative, interest. For if we know what the traditional picaresque is about, and we see that Ralph Ellison's novel is truly picaresque, then we may have enlarged this novel's meaning. Viewed one way, the book is simply a novel about the problems of Negroes. But from another perspective, we see, the book has wider appeal and wider meaning. It is a picaresque novel—that is to say, an expression of a certain essential and unending chaos in life.

Notes

NOTES TO INTRODUCTION

1. For example, G. E. Alvarez. *Le Thème de la femme dans la picaresque espagnole* (Groningen, 1955); and Erik von Kraemer, *Le Type du faux mendiant dans les littératures romanes depuis le moyen âge jusqu'au XVII* siècle* (Helsingfors, 1944).

2. See the many studies of separate picaresque novels such as *Moll Flanders, Lazarillo de Tormes,* etc.

3. The dominant type of study of the genre, e.g., Alberto del Monte, *Itinerario del romanzo picaresco spagnolo* (Firenze, 1957); F. W. Chandler, *The Literature of Roguery, 1* (New York, 1907; reprinted 1958), and his *Romances of Roguery: An Episode in the History of the Novel, Part I, The Picaresque Novel in Spain* (London, 1899); Fonger de Haan, *An Outline of the History of the Novela Picaresca in Spain* (The Hague, 1903); Robert Alter, *The Rogue's Progress: Studies in the Picaresque Novel* (Cambridge, Mass., 1964). Numerous other references to histories of the genre can be found in Del Monte's exhaustive bibliographical notes and in the "Introducción" and the bibliography of Michel Robert Ramon's *Nueva Interpretación del pícaro y de la novela picaresca española hecha a base de un estudio de las tres obras maestras del género* (Ann Arbor, 1957). Ramon's work has an extensive and able survey of the criticism of the genre in its "Introducción." It has been thought unnecessary to repeat such a survey here.

4. Claudio Guillén's "Toward a Definition of the Picaresque," *Proceedings of the IIIrd Congress of the International Comparative Literature Association* (The Hague, 1962), despite its great learning and real insight, is too tentative a definition, and too unsystematic. Most defini-

tions of the picaresque novel remain loose collections of adjectives such as "realistic," "comic," "episodic," "roguish," and the like.

NOTES TO PART ONE

1. René Wellek and Austin Warren, *Theory of Literature* (New York, 1949), p. 222.

2. See the chapter, "Realism and the Novel Form," in his book, *The Rise of the Novel: Studies in Defoe, Richardson and Fielding* (Berkeley and Los Angeles, 1959). It should be added that the great realistic novels of the nineteenth century, e.g., *Middlemarch,* used the probable-causal plot in a new, elaborate way—demonstrating the intricacy of the web that binds reality in causal order.

3. This is a good place to explain the system of documentation that will obtain throughout. Citations in the text will refer to specific translations of foreign works or English originals; the originals of foreign works have been cited in the notes. The translations of English originals cited in the text are:

Lazarillo de Tormes, trans. Mack Hendricks Singleton, in *Masterpieces of the Spanish Golden Age,* ed. Angel Flores (New York, 1957), pp. 25-84. This will be cited in the text merely by its page number.

Thomas Nashe, *The Unfortunate Traveller,* in *Elizabethan Fiction,* ed. Robert Ashley and Edwin M. Moseley (New York, 1956), pp. 203-308. This will be cited in the text merely by its page number.

Mateo Alemán, *The Rogue, or the Life of Guzmán de Alfarache,* trans. James Mabbe, 4 vols. (London, 1924), cited in the text merely by volume and page number.

Francisco de Quevedo, *The Life and Adventures of Don Pablos the Sharper,* trans. by "divers hands," rev. and ed. Mack Hendricks Singleton, in *Masterpieces of the Spanish Golden Age,* ed. Angel Flores (New York, 1957), pp. 85-233. This translation of *El Buscón* is cited merely by its page number.

Hans Jacob Christoffels von Grimmelshausen, *Simplicissimus The Vagabond . . . ,* trans. A. T. S. Goodrick (London, 1924). This is cited merely by its page number.

Alain René Le Sage, *The History of Gil Blas of Santillana,* trans. Henri van Laun, rev. Henri Roberts, 3 vols. (Philadelphia, 1898). In Part One, the first Roman number in a citation refers to the volume of the edition, the following Arabic number to the "book" in the novel, the following Roman number to the chapter in the "book," and the final Arabic number to the page in the volume of the edition. In the following Parts, such complete citation has seemed unnecessary. Therefore only the volume and page number of the *edition* are cited by an italicized Arabic number and an Arabic number without italics in the usual manner.

Notes

Daniel Defoe, *Moll Flanders,* intro. by Godfrey Davies (New York, 1949). This will be cited in the text merely by its page number.

Tobias Smollett, *The Adventures of Roderick Random,* ed. George Saintsbury, 3 vols, (London, 1895). This will be cited in the text merely by volume and page number.

The originals of foreign works cited in the notes are:

La Vie de Lazarillo de Tormès (*La Vida de Lazarillo de Tormes*), trans. A. Morel-Fatio, with introduction by Marcel Bataillon (Paris, 1958). This will be cited in the notes as "Bataillon," followed by a page number.

Mateo Alemán, *Guzmán de Alfarache,* ed. Samuel Gili y Gaya, 5 vols. (Madrid, 1942-50). This will be cited in the notes as "Gili," followed by the volume and page numbers.

Francisco de Quevedo Villegas, *La Vida del Buscón,* in *Obras completas en prosa,* ed. Luis Astrana Marín, 3rd ed. (Madrid, 1945), pp. 115-79. This will be cited in the notes as "Astrana," followed by a page number.

Hans Jacob Christoffels von Grimmelshausen, *Grimmelshausens Werke,* Vols. 1 and 2: *Der abentheurliche Simplicius Simplicissimus,* ed. Felix Bobertag, Deutsche National-Litteratur, Vols. 33 and 34 (Berlin and Stuttgart, n.d.). This will be cited in the notes as "Bobertag," followed by the volume and page numbers.

Alain René Le Sage, *Histoire de Gil Blas de Santillane,* ed. Maurice Bardon, 2 vols. (Paris, 1955). This will be cited in the notes as "Bardon," followed by the volume and page numbers.

4. Gili, *1,* 178: "Era la suya una de las más perfectas y peregrina hermosura que en otra se había visto."

5. Gili, *1,* 180: "Sus calidades muy conformes a las de Daraja: mancebo rico, galán, discreto y, sobre todo, valiente y animoso. . . ."

6. See his *The Anatomy of Criticism* (Princeton, 1957), pp. 163 ff.

7. The Spanish original, as often, is less fulsome. Gili, *1,* 240: "las partes acusasen y fuesen malintencionados los actores, los muertos y heridos muchos."

8. Gili, *1,* 242: "ya tenían hecha relación a sus Altezas de todo el caso."

9. The king and queen are the romance's perpetual embodiment of beneficent Providence. Compare the "recurrent Dickens figure, the Good Rich Man," that Orwell discovers in his essay on Dickens in George Orwell, *A Collection of Essays* (Garden City, N. Y., 1954), p. 59.

10. In the picaresque novel there is little of the orderly change of character that is the peculiar forte of the realistic novel. See Carl Grabo, *The Technique of the Novel* (New York, 1928), pp. 217-18: "The characteristic theme of fiction is the alteration of human personality under the pressure of circumstance."

11. Bobertag, *2,* 85-86: "hinckte ein Kerl an einem Stecken in der Hand in die Stube, der hatte einen verbundenen Kopff, einen Arm in

der Schlinge und so elend Kleider an, dass ich ihm keinen Heller darum geben hätte."

12. The dance-pattern re-encounters with the cornet (p. 261) and Oliver (p. 272) are also inconsequential, implying a lack of order and stability in the world.

13. The introduction of the finding of lost parents into the structure of *Moll Flanders* and *Roderick Random* is probably a flaw in these novels. This problem will be discussed at the end of Part Three, where it will be convenient to take up the difficult problem of how an author can successfully *end* a novel about chaos.

14. Bobertag, *2,* 124: "Hieraus vernahm ich umständlich, dass ich meines Einsiedlers und des Gubernator Ramsay Schwester leiblicher Sohn gewesen, aber ach leider viel zu spät, dann meine Eltern waren beyde tod, und von meinem Vetter Ramsay konte ich anders nichts erfahren, als dass die Hanauer ihn mit samt der Schwedischen Guarnison ausgeschafft hätten, wesswegen er dann vor Zorn und Ungedult gantz unsinnig worden wäre."

Another motif that would seem, at first sight, to give a sense of stability in *Simplicissimus* is the prophecy pattern. This is part of the novel's background of divination and magic but in no way alters our sense of the chaos of events. Events can be prophesied by wizards and witches in this novel, but we never feel that they are ordered or predictable in any important way. Compare the feel of events ordered by gods in epic literature and events predictable by characters in the "realistic" novel.

15. Some other dance patterns that help solidify the chaotic picaresque plot in *Gil Blas* are the meetings with Fabricio (I, 1, xvii; II, 8, xiii; III, 11, x), with Tordesillas and Cogollos (II, 7, iii; III, 9, iv ff.; III, 11, xiii), and the whole pattern of meetings with Don Alphonso (particularly II, 4, ix ff.; III, 9, ii; III, 9, x).

16. This pattern had already appeared in *Le Roman comique* and *Le Diable boiteux*. These works belong to the literature of roguery but are not usually considered classic picaresque novels and hence are not treated here.

17. Critics who see the picaresque novel as rising from one particular socioeconomic historical situation apparently are mistaken. The genre seems to arise from a multiplicity of such situations, and the chaotic world it expresses is not merely a historical one, but eternal.

18. It is shown in Part Two, where the novel's characterization is treated, that the picaresque is only one strain in *Roderick Random*.

19. See the Preface in the edition cited, *1,* xli.

20. Gili, *1,* 107: "A mí me comenzaron a venir y me siguieron, sin dar un momento de espacio desde que comencé a caminar, y así en todas partes nunca me faltaron."

21. Gili, *3*, 162: "como sin juicio."

22. Point of view is fully discussed in Part Three.

23. Gili, *3*, 169: "Con estas exclamaciones pasaba perdido y con mi poca prudencia. . . ."

24. Astrana, 130: "Pero cuando comienzan desgracias en uno, parece que nunca se han de acabar, que andan encadenadas y unas traen a otras."

25. Astrana, 131: "Y no hacía a solas sino considerar cómo casi era peor lo que había pasado en Alcalá en un día que todo lo que me sucedió con Cabra."

26. Bobertag, *2*, 132: "Ich betrachtete, was vor Veränderung ich seithero erduldet. Da stellete ich mir vor Augen, dass ich an eben dem selbigen Ort den Anfang gemachet, aus einem freyen Kerl zu einem Knecht der Liebe zu werden, dass ich seithero aus einem Officier ein Baur, aus einem reichen Baur ein armer Edelmann, aus einem Simplicio ein Melchior, aus einem Witwer ein Ehemann, aus einem Ehemann ein Gauch und aus einem Gauch wieder ein Witwer worden wäre; Item, dass ich aus eines Baurs Sohn zu einem Sohn eines rechtschaffenen Soldaten und gleichwol wieder zu einem Sohn meines Knäns worden."

27. Violence and pain are "realistically" portrayed elsewhere in fiction, e.g., in the *Iliad*, but the ugly, brutish, and disgusting elements are largely kept out of sight in such non-picaresque fiction.

28. Gili, *4*, 137-38: "La fortuna, que ni es fuerte ni una, sino flaca y varia, comenzó a mostrarnos la poca constancia suya. . . ."

29. Gili, *4*, 217: "Pasaba en ella [una casa] y con mi pobreza como un Fúcar. Y así acabara, si mi corta fortuna y suerte avarienta no me salieran a el encuentro, viniéndose a juntar el tramposo con el codicioso."

30. Gili, *3*, 267: "Concluyo aquí con decir que, cuando la desdicha sigue a un hombre, ninguna diligencia ni buen consejo le aprovecha, pues de donde creí traer lana volví sin ella trasquilado."

31. Gili, *3*, 281: "Mas el hombre propone y Dios dispone. No son éstas las costas de ¡quién pensara!, porque no se puede previnir una pedrada que acaso tiró un loco y mató con ella, ni ser adevinos de cosas tan desproporcionadas a el entendimiento." "Fortune" is named everywhere in *Guzmán*, e.g., Mabbe, *4*, 126, 153, 181-82, 220, 221, 229, 315, 327, 333, 349, *et passim*.

32. Astrana 179: "Yo, que vi que duraba mucho este negocio, y más la fortuna en perseguirme. . . ."

33. An example of the identification of the picaresque world in the novels with *the* world is the advice of Pablos' father: "He who does not steal in this world cannot survive" (p. 87). Astrana, 118: "Quien no hurta en el mundo no vive."

34. References to Fortune or *Glück,* and to the instability of good fortune, are found on pp. 27, 35, 45, 108, 139, 149-50, 310, 313, 353, *et passim* in the English translation. These pages correspond respectively in Bobertag to: *1,* 39, 48, 61, 142, 179, 192; *2,* 103, 106, 177.

35. Bobertag, *1,* 220: "die bekandte Waarsagerin zu Soest rieth und mich versicherte, dass ich mehr Feinde in derselben Stadt und unter meinem Regiment als ausserhalb und in den feindlichen Guarnisonen hätte, die mir und meinem Geld nachstelleten."

36. Bobertag, *1,* 236: "Also ward ich bey Zeiten gewahr, dass nichts beständigers in der Welt ist als die Unbeständigkeit selbsten. Dahero muste ich sorgen, wann das Glück einmal seine Mucken gegen mich auslasse, dass es mir meine jetzige Wolfahrt gewaltig einträncken würde."

37. Bobertag, *1,* 240: "Meine Hoffart vermehrete sich mit meinem Glück, daraus endlich nichts anders als mein Fall erfolgen konte." Other statements in which such dire predictions or foreshadowings of a fall from his success are made can be found in the English translation on pp. 193, 202, 210, 217-18, 230, 231, *et passim.* The corresponding pages in Bobertag are *1,* 249, 260, 269, 278-79, 294, 295.

38. Other instances of events dominated by Fortune are to be found, in the English edition, on pp. 28-29, 39, 44, 45, 86, 137, 231, 250-51, 255, 338-39, *et passim.*

39. References to the power of Fortune occur throughout *Gil Blas,* though more of them are found in the second half than in the first. See the English edition, *2,* 232, 241, 255, 298, 301; *3,* 13, 52, 80, 274, 292, 304, *et passim.* The corresponding pages in Bardon are *2,* 2, 8, 18, 48, 51, 88, 116, 136, 271, 284, 292.

40. Bardon, *2,* 177: "Vous ne serez plus le jouet de la fortune. Je veux vous affranchir de son pouvoir en vous rendant maître d'un bien qu'elle ne pourra vous ôter."

41. Bardon, *2,* 80: "Après avoir tant de fois éprouvé que la fortune ne m'avait pas plus tôt renversé qu'elle me relevait, je n'aurais dû regarder l'état fâcheux où j'étais que comme une occasion prochaine de prospérité."

42. That is, it never seems satisfied until "The End" of the novel. See note 13 above.

43. It is not untypical of the novels we are considering that a pure chance occurrence should plunge the hero into a latrine. The picaresque novelist often seems to equate life seen as disordered accident with feces.

44. Astrana, 171: "Entraron en mi aposento; y como me vieron en la cama, y a ella conmigo, cerraron conmigo y con ella, y diéronme cuatro o seis empellones muy grandes, y arrastráronme fuera de la cama . . . el amigo, que era un frutero que estaba en el aposento de adentro, dió a correr. Ellos, que lo vieron, y supieron (por lo que decía otro güésped de

casa) que yo no lo era, arrancaron tras el picaño y asiéronle, y dejáronme a mí repelado y apuñeado."

45. Bardon, *1,* 113: "Je marchais à tâtons dans la rue; et j'avais fait peut-être la moitié de mon chemin, lorsque d'une fenêtre on me coiffa d'une cassolette qui ne chatouillait point l'odorat. Je puis dire même que je n'en perdis rien, tant je fus bien ajusté!"

46. Bardon, *1,* 122: "et je m'en acquittai si bien, qu'un voisin qui rentrait chez lui, me prenant pour un de ces animaux dont j'imitais les miaulements, ramassa un caillou qui se trouva sous ses pieds, et me le jeta de toute sa force, en distant: Maudit soit le matou! Je reçus le coup à la tête, et j'en fus si étourdi dans le moment, que je pensai tomber à la renverse. Je sentis que, j'étais bien blessé. Il ne m'en fallut pas davantage pour me dégoûter de la galanterie. . . ."

47. This is again the implication of another "accident" that happens to Moll a little later. This second accident is a variation of the one we have just described:

> It happened that while I was going along the street in Covent Garden, there was a great cry of "Stop thief! Stop thief!" Some artists had, it seems, put a trick upon a shopkeeper, and being pursued, some of them fled one way and some another; and one of them was, they said, dressed up in widow's weeds, upon which the mob gathered about me, and some said I was the person, others said no. Immediately came the mercer's journeyman, and he swore aloud I was the person, and so seized on me [pp. 248-49].

Instead of Moll's committing a crime and another criminal's being seized (as in the previous incident cited), another criminal commits a crime, and Moll is seized. Again, events have so contrived things as to have two thieves in one spot. Again the feeling of chaos that such a reversal of probability brings turns upon an image of a dark London saturated with criminals. Criminality, commitment to disorder, almost seems to employ more people than middle-class lawfulness.

NOTES TO PART TWO

1. I am aware that the following discussion of the comic hero is oversimplified, but it may help in describing the character of the typical picaro.

2. See his famous definition in Maynard Mack, ed., *Joseph Andrews* (New York, 1948), pp. xiii-xiv. Cited in W. K. Wimsatt, Jr., and Cleanth Brooks, *Literary Criticism: A Short History* (New York, 1957), p. 49.

3. This statement is true of even such complicated comic figures as Falstaff. Regardless of his complications, he too is defined. The name "Falstaff" calls to mind a very definite personality indeed.

4. See Part One, p. 10.

5. Thomas McFarland, "Antony and Octavius," *Yale Review, 48* (1959), 204-28.

6. See W. K. Wimsatt's discussion of this traditional distinction in his *The Verbal Icon: Studies in the Meaning of Poetry* (Lexington, Ky., 1954), pp. 77-79.

7. Lazarillo's origins are chaotic in the fragmentation of his family: his father dies, his mother takes on a Moorish stable hand, and Lazarillo's brother is their bastard.

8. Gili, *1*, 39: "la figura inconstante deste discurso."

9. Gili, *1*, 93: "Ambos me conocieron por hijo: el uno me lo llamaba y el otro también."

10. Gili, *1*, 94-95: "Por suyo me llamo, por tal me tengo, pues de aquella melonada quedé legitimado con el santo matrimonio y estáme muy mejor, antes que diga un cualquiera que soy malnacido y hijo de ninguno."

11. The Spanish has simply, "Sea como fuere y el levantisco, mi padre . . ." (Gili, *1*, 94). The Mabbe citation does, however, sum up the real doubt in the novel about the merchant's background.

12. Gili, *1*, 98: "Si mi madre enredó dos, mi abuela dos docenas. . . ."

13. Gili, *1*, 98: "Con esta hija enredó cien linajes, diciendo y jurando a cada padre que era suya; y a todos les parecía: a cuál en los ojos, a cuál en la boca. . . ."

14. Gili, *1*, 99: "creía, por algunas indirectas, haber sido hija de un caballero, deudo cercano a los duques de Medinasidonia."

15. It is possible, too, that these accounts of a picaro's chaotic origins contribute to the generally unsettling effects picaresque novels have on readers. For if the reader doesn't happen to resemble both his parents very closely, then for him, as for the picaro, the basic facts of his life may be shrouded in uncertainty. Potentially, there is a shock effect for the reader at the very beginning of picaresque novels as unsettling as those produced by the rapid event sequence and other devices.

One should note carefully the symbolic or metaphoric meaning of the picaro's origins. It may be that certain men in sixteenth- and seventeenth-century Spain were uncertain of their origins (as other scholars have noted), but these facts do not diminish the role of the picaro's origins in the novels themselves. The symbolic usefulness of the device to the purpose of the picaresque novelist is attested to by its employment in German and English novels presumably rising out of different historical circumstances.

16. Gili, *1*, 100: "Yo fuí desgraciado . . . quedé solo, sin árbol que me hiciese sombra."

17. Astrana, 119: "¿Eso sabes decir? No serás bobo . . . esas cosas, aunque sean verdad, no se han de decir."

18. See Alberto del Monte, *L'Itinerario del romanzo picaresco spagnolo* (Firenze, 1957), p. 54 *et passim.*

19. These qualities are discussed later in this Part.

20. This lack of focus on the hero can best be substantiated by citing a representative part of the table of contents. Bardon, *1,* 405:

> Chap. III. Du grand changement qui arriva chez don Vincent, et de l'étrange résolution que l'amour fit prendre à la belle Aurore.
> Chap. IV. LE MARIAGE DE VENGEANCE (Nouvelle).
> Chap. V. De ce que fit Aurore de Guzman, lorsqu'elle fut à Salamanque.
> Chap. VI. Quelles ruses Aurore mit en usage pour se faire aimer de don Luis Pacheco.
> Chap. VII. Gil Blas change de condition, et il passe au service de don Gonzale Pacheco.
> Chap. VIII. De quel caractère était la marquise de Chaves, et quelles personnes allaient ordinairement chez elle.

21. Bardon, *1,* 277: "Je suis fils d'une comédienne de Madrid, fameuse par sa déclamation, et plus encore par ses galanteries; elle se nommait Lucinde. Pour un père, je ne puis sans témérité m'en donner un."

22. See pp. 56 ff.

23. See *The Rise of the Novel,* especially the chapter, "Realism and the Novel Form."

24. See *Moll Flanders,* p. 38.

25. Del Monte, p. 70: "La psicologia di Guzmán infatti è condizionata dall'incontro iniziale con una società ostile, crudele e fraudolenta, contro cui egli reagisce adottandone quegli stessi vizi che ne condanna."

26. Bataillon, 98: "siendo ciego, me alumbró y adestró en la carrera de vivir."

27. Jack Wilton differs from most picaresque heroes in undergoing no picaresque education. When we first meet him, he is already an adult experienced in the world's ways and ready to trick whomever he can. But since the world he lives in is rife with trickery, we must admit that all Jack is doing is playing the world's game. Even the noble and pure Surrey can "counterfeit most daintily" (p. 245).

28. Gili, *1,* 101: "salí a ver mundo, peregrinando por él, encomendándome a Dios y buenas gentes en quien hice confianza."

29. Gili, *1,* 104-5: "donde la comida falta, no hay bien que llegue ni mal que no sobre, gusto que dure ni contento que asista: todos riñen sin saber por qué. . . . No supe qué hacer. . . . Hallábame entre miedos y esperanzas. . . . Anduve vacilando. . . ."

30. Gili, *1*, 206: "sin saber dónde estaba, que aun me parecía cosa de sueño."

31. Gili, *1*, 109: "chapetón . . . un Juan de buen alma."

32. Gili, *1*, 120: "Vi el cielo abierto. El me pareció un ángel. . . ."

33. Gili, *1*, 245: "Aun este trago me quedaba por pasar. . . ."

34. Gili, *2*, 9: "acusado de ladrón en profecía."

35. Gili, *2*, 18: "Allí supe adobar la cebada con agua caliente, que creciese un tercio, y medir falso. . . ."

36. Gili, *2*, 20: "algunos noveles."

37. Gili, *2*, 54: "Es cuento largo tratar desto. Todo anda revuelto, todo apriesa, todo marañado. No hallarás hombre con hombre; todos vivimos en asechanza los unos de los otros, como el gato para el ratón o la araña para la culebra, que hallándola descuidada, se deja colgar de un hilo y, asiéndola de la cerviz, la aprieta fuertemente, no apartándose della hasta que con su ponzoña la mata."

38. See note 33 to Part One.

39. Astrana, 128: "Hiciéronle creer que estaba endemoniado. . . ."

40. Astrana, 128: "Señor nuevo, a pocas estrenas como ésta, envejecerá."

41. Astrana, 131: " 'Haz como vieres,' dice el refrán, y dice bien. De puro considerar en él, vine a resolverme de ser bellaco con los bellacos, y más, si pudiese, que todos."

42. Bobertag, *1*, 10: "dann ich kante weder Gott noch Menschen, weder Himmel noch Hölle, weder Engel noch Teuffel und wuste weder Gutes noch Böses zuunterscheiden . . . ich vermittelst solcher Theologiä wie unsere erste Eltern im Paradiss gelebet. . . ."

43. Bobertag, *1*, 31: "Gleichwol aber ist die pure Einfalt, gegen andern Menschen zurechnen, noch immerzu bey mir verblieben, dahero der Einsidel (weil weder er, noch ich, meinin rechten Namen gewust) mich nur Simplicium genennet."

44. Bobertag, *1*, 37: "sich selbst erkennen, böse Gesellschafft meiden und beständig verbleiben."

45. Bobertag, *1*, 64: "Meines Erachtens ist er durch Lesung vieler Papistischen Bücher von dem Leben der Alten Eremiten . . . hierzu verleitet worden."

46. Bobertag, *1*, 69-70: "nichts als eitel Greuel," "fand ich eitel Heucheley," "unzehlbare Thorheiten."

47. Bobertag, *1*, 71: "Ich aber schwieg still. . . ."

48. Bobertag, *1*, 85: "Die anwesende Herren . . . nanten meine That, die ich aus Einfalt begangen, eine Wunderkluge Erfindung und Vorbedeutung künfftiger Dapfferkeit und unerschrockenen Resolution. . . ."

49. Bobertag, *1,* 109: "achte und glaube nicht alles, was man dich überreden will, und stelle dich doch, als wann du alles glaubtest."

50. Bobertag, *1,* 112-13: "gedencke, du habst Victori genug, wann du in deiner Jugend drey abgefäumte alte Vetteln, mit denen man den Teufel im weiten Feld fangen möchte, betrügen kanst; du kanst aus dieser Occasion Hofnung schöpffen, bey zunehmenden Jahren und künfftigen im Alter mehrers zu leisten."

51. Bobertag *1,* 116: "ich habe die Probe des Feuers überstanden und bin darinn gehärtet worden; jetzt wollen wir probiren, welcher den andern am besten agiren wird können."

52. Bardon, *1,* 10-11: "loin de m'exhorter à ne tromper personne, ils devaient me recommander de ne pas me laisser duper."

53. Bardon, *1,* 22-23: "Eh! voit-on d'autres gens dans le monde? Non, mon ami, tous les hommes aiment à s'approprier le bien d'autrui; c'est un sentiment général, la manière seule de le faire en est différente. Les conquérants, par exemple. . . . Les personnes de qualité empruntent, et ne rendent point. Les banquiers, trésoriers, agents de change, commis, et tous les marchands, tant gros que petits, ne sont pas fort scrupuleux. Pour les gens de justice . . . on n'ignore point ce qu'ils savent faire."

54. Bardon, *2,* 172: "Je me proposai . . . si jamais je sortais de prison, d'acheter une chaumière et d'y aller vivre en philosophe."

55. Bataillon, 106: "yo siempre le llevaba por los peores caminos, y adrede, por le hacer más daño. Si había piedras, por ellas; si lodo, por lo más alto; que, aunque yo no iba por lo más enjuto, holgábame a mí de quebrar un ojo, por quebrar dos al que ninguno tenía."

56. Gili, *2,* 183: "Ordenanzas Mendicativas."

57. Gili, *2,* 206: "Teníamos una vida, que los verdaderamente senadores —y aun comedores—, nosotros éramos: que aunque no tan respetados, la pasábamos mas reposada, mejor y de menos pesadumbre. . . ."

58. Gili, *2,* 194: "Verdad es que me escaldaron; mas no tanto como lo acriminaba."

59. Gili, *2,* 197: "Responde con humildad a las malas palabras y con blandas a las ásperas. . . ."

60. Gili, *2,* 197: "Demás desto, enseñóme a fingir lepra, hacer llagas, hinchar una pierna, tullir un brazo, teñir el color del rostro, alterar todo el cuerpo y otros primores curiosos del arte. . . ."

61. Gili, *2,* 269: "Esa es la ciencia—le respondí—que estando de otra fáciles de ser abiertos, ni grado ni gracias. En las dificultades han de conocerse los ingenios . . . no . . . [en] cosas agibles, de suyo ya hechas."

62. Astrana, 134: "Yo, que me vi ya mal con la ama, y que no la podía burlar, busqué nuevas trazas de holgarme. . . ."

63. Bobertag *1,* 207, 211: "Also machte ichs aller Orten und überkam dadurch einen grossen Ruff"; "ich Ehre, Ruhm und Gunst in Hand-

lungen suchte und auch gefunden, die sonst bey andern wären Straff-würdig gewesen"; "Ich war (wie bereits erwehnet) so beflissen, Ehre und Ruhm zu erjagen, dass ich auch nicht davor schlaffen konte, und wann ich so Grillen hatte und manche Nacht lag, neue Fündigen und List zu ersinnen. . . ."

64. Bardon, *1*, 23: "vous devez plutôt vous réjouir de vous voir ici. Vous êtes jeune, et vous paraissez facile; vous vous seriez bientôt perdu dans le monde. Vous y auriez indubitablement rencontré des libertins qui vous auraient engagé dans toutes sortes de débauches, au lieu que votre innocence se trouve ici dans un port assuré."

65. Bataillon, 142: "desde que viví con el ciego, la tenia tan hecha bolsa, que me acaeció tener en ella doce o quince maravedís, todo en medias blancas, sin que me estorbase el comer. Porque de otra manera no era señor de una blanca que el maldito ciego no cayese con ella. . . ."

66. Gili, *4*, 19: "Fuí muy gentil caleta, buzo, cuatrero, maleador y mareador, pala, ploeo, escolta, estafa y zorro."

67. Gili, *2*, 83: "No puse los ojos en mí, sino en los otros. Parecióme lícito lo que ellos hacían. . . ."

68. Gili, *3*, 89-90: "continuamente andaba solícito, buscando lo necesario a el oficio que ya profesaba, para ir con ello ganando tierra y rindiendo los gustos al mío."

69. Gili, *4*, 92: "Ya no se juzgan almas ni más de aquello que ven los ojos."

70. These remarks on tragedy owe much to the article by Thomas McFarland cited in note 5 to Part Two, and to Albert Cook's *The Dark Voyage and the Golden Mean: A Philosophy of Comedy* (Cambridge, Mass., 1949).

71. The phrase, and to some extent the notion, "implied author," is taken from Wayne Booth's *The Rhetoric of Fiction* (Chicago, 1962).

72. Don Quixote is the best example of this, especially in the Don's and Sancho's final switching of sides. The idea that comedy reconciles us to the way things are is found in Hesse's *Steppenwolf* and earlier in German romantic theory. See Wimsatt and Brooks, *A Short History*, Chapter 17.

73. In some of his protean changes, Simplicissimus shows almost a comic vitality; see the discussion of the comic hero in Chapter 18 of Susanne Langer's *Feeling and Form, A Theory of Art, Developed from "Philosophy in a New Key"* (New York, 1953). But comic mastery of life's circumstances is really only incidental in *Simplicissimus,* and any comic joy is continually dampened; see above, p. 31. Comic passages, just like the interpolated romances in *Guzmán,* may have been inserted into picaresque novels to relieve a dark tone that otherwise might have been too monotonously oppressive to keep the reader reading.

Notes

74. Bobertag, *1*, 102: "Packe dich nur geschwind aus dem Bette und trolle dich aus dem Haus, damit ich nicht samt dir in deines Herrn Ungnade komme, wann man dich bey mir findet."

75. Bobertag, *1*, 107: "Er wünschte, dass ihm der Teufel den Hals in tausend Stücken breche, ehe er in die Vestung käme! So bald er ihn aber eingelassen und auff der innern Fallbrücke bewillkommte, fehlte wenig oder gar nichts, dass er ihm nicht selbst an Stegraiff griff, seine Devotion gegen ihm zu bezeugen. . . ."

76. Bobertag, *1*, 107: "was vor ein Wunder-falscher Geist regiret doch die Menschen."

77. Bobertag, *1*, 264: "beflisse ich mich der Bescheidenheit."

78. Bobertag, *1*, 281: "jedermans Freundschafft zu behalten, so lang ich noch in derselbigen Vestung zu verbleiben . . . willens war."

79. Simplicissimus' hermit father is obviously a parallel to the corrupt worldly cleric, the pastor. Thus, Simplicissimus learns steadfastness from the hermit; he is corrupted into personal chaos by the pastor; finally, in the original ending to the book, he decides to return to the original lessons of the hermit, who is revealed, at the last, to be both his spiritual and fleshly father.

80. Bardon, *2*, 183: "Quelque envie que j'eusse de rire en entendant une si comique déclamation, j'eus la force d'y résister; je fis plus, je déclamai contre le kermès sans savoir ce que c'était, et donnai au diable, à tout hasard, ceux qui l'ont inventé."

81. Bataillon, 96: "no por mozo, sino por hijo."

82. Bataillon, 96: "solo soy."

83. Bataillon, 120: "No supe más lo que Dios dél hizo, ni curé de lo saber."

84. Bataillon, 170: "Con todo, le quería bien, con ver que no tenía ni podía más. . . ."

85. Compare the novel's criticism of the Utopian Erasmus and More, p. 235.

86. That is, the end of Chapter iii, Book II, Part I, of the novel, or Mabbe, *1*, 269.

87. Erich Fromm, *The Art of Loving* (New York, 1956), p. 9.

88. In his loneliness and lack of love, Pablos, *el Buscón,* reveals much the same outer and inner chaos that Guzmán does. His lack of support from his family reveals the chaos in society: his parents are hanged; his only relative and guardian has no understanding for Pablos and was his father's hangman! Don Pedro is no friend to him, first tricking him, then having his face slashed. Picaresque society dissolves when Pablos deserts his thieving friends in prison and when he is robbed by his "friends,"

the Licentiate Brandalagas and Pero López. Finally, Pablos' attentions to a nun are only a weird parody of love.

89. Bobertag, *1*, 74-75: "nirgends fand sich mehr Neid, Hass, Missgunst, Hader und Zanck, als zwischen Brüdern, Schwestern und andern angebornen Freunden . . . hasste das Handwerck aller Orten einander . . . Mancher Herr schund seine getreue Diener und Unterthanen, hingegen wurden etliche Unterthanen an ihren frommen Herren zu Schelmen."

90. Gili, *2*, 74: "La locura y desvanecimiento de los hombres, como te decía, los trae perdidos en vanidades. . . ."

91. Gili, *2*, 100: "Con quanto gané, jugué y hurté, ni compré juro, censo, casa ni capa o cosa con que me cubijar." The translation is a bit faulty here.

92. Gili, *2*, 101-2: "Mas no pude ya otra cosa. No sé qué puede ser, que deseando ser buenos nunca lo somos, y aunque por horas lo proponemos, en años nunca lo cumplimos ni en toda la vida salimos con ello."

93. Another confession of instability in moral resolves is found on p. 250, Volume Two, of the Mabbe translation; Gili, *2*, 281.

94. Gili, *3*, 192: "¡Qué buena resolucíon, si duraral"

95. Gili, *3*, 250: "Salí de Roma con determinacíon de ser hombre de bien. . . . Fe sin obras es fe muerta."

96. Gili, *4*, 151: "Mas a la casta Dorotea, ni las partes deste poder del teniente ni pasiones de los más le hacían el menor sentimiento del mundo. . . . Mostrábase a todos estos combates fortísima peña inexpugnable. . . ."

97. Gili, *2*, 224: "por curiosidad quise ir a ver si su caridad y limosna igualaba con la de Roma."

98. Gili, *2*, 193: "Quise ver lo que a tales horas podía sacar, sólo por curiosidad."

99. Gili, *1*, 116: "siempre los mozos se despeñan tras el gusto presente, sin respetar ni mirar el daño venidero."

100. Gili, *5*, 48: "que faltarle un punto de su ordinario, es un punto que se suelta de una calza de aguja, que por allí se va toda."

101. Gili, *2*, 257: "las malas mañas que aprendí, me quedaron indelebles."

102. Gili, *2*, 278: "Yo no lo estoy . . . de mí mesmo ni del que se les podría hacer . . . soy hijo de Eva. . . ."

103. Gili, *3*, 70: "A mí me parece que son todos los hombres como yo, flacos, faciles, con pasiones naturales y aun extrañas." *El Buscón* does not go as far in revealing internal instability of character because the book lacks the introspection of *Guzmán*. This lack of introspection is typical of shorter picaresque novels like *Lazarillo, The Unfortunate*

Traveller, and *El Buscón.* Only in the longer picaresque does it seem possible to do complete justice to the character's internal instability. Nevertheless, we feel considerable instability in Pablos because of the contradiction between his resolves and actions. He aspires early in the book to be a virtuous gentleman (pp. 87-88; Astrana, 118), but at Alcalá he decides to "be a knave among knaves" (p. 117; Astrana, 131). He renews his resolve when he receives his inheritance (p. 130; Astrana, 136) but abandons it when he embraces the life of roguery in Madrid. There is no reason given for the capricious change. When he abandons his role as successful playwright, again it is a capricious decision: "my only concern was to take some time out and have a good time" (p. 224; Astrana, 175). His becoming a wooer of nuns is again largely a gratuitous decision, as is his taking up with a group of thugs at the end. Pablos has degenerated from a person with fixed aims and ideals to a picaro unable to control his impulses.

104. See pp. 25 and 40 of the English translation, and see also above, p. 60.

105. Bobertag, *2*, 38: "als ob ich wieder ein Einsidel werden, meine Sünden büssen und der Barmhertzigkeit Gottes vor meine hoffende Erlösung biss in mein Ende dancken wolte."

106. Bobertag, *2*, 80: "Indem ich mich nun selbst so marterte und quälete und doch nichts entschliessen konte. . . ."

107. Bobertag, *2*, 133: "Ja ich nahm mir vor, zu philosophiren und mich eines gottseligen Lebens zu befleissen. . . ."

108. Bobertag *2*, 168: "Mit solchen und dergleichen Worten machte er mir das Maul gantz wässerig. . . ."

109. Bobertag, *2*, 187: "wie mein Vatter seel. biss an mein Ende darinn verharren werde." For other examples of this schism see pp. 277ff., and p. 308 in the English translation.

110. Bobertag, *1*, 258: "Ich bekam von ihm wol närrische Anschläge und seltzame Grillen ins Hirn. . . ."

111. The German hero is of course a version of the romance hero described above.

112. Bardon, *1*, 49: "ce que je lui pardonnai volontiers."

113. Compare also the smooth compromises Gil Blas makes in his easygoing morality: he prays God to forgive his sins with Dr. Sangrado but keeps his earnings (*1*, 144); he regrets the theft from Master Simon but keeps his loot (*2*, 240).

114. Bardon, *2*, 90: "*Songe que tu es présentement au roi:* ces paroles que le duc m'avait dites s'offraient sans cesse à ma mémoire, et devenaient des semences d'ambition qui germaient d'instant en instant dans mon esprit."

115. Bardon, *2*, 96: "Comment aurais-je pu, après cela, ne me pas croire un homme de conséquence?"

116. Bardon, *2*, 141: "moins peut-être par amitié que par ostentation."

117. Bardon, *2*, 135: "L'avarice et l'ambition qui me possédaient changèrent entièrement mon humeur. Je perdis toute ma gaieté; je devins distrait et rêveur, en un mot, un sot animal."

118. Bardon, *2*, 135: "En vérité, Gil Blas, je ne te reconnais plus. Avant que tu fusses à la cour, tu avais toujours l'esprit tranquille. A présent je te vois, sans cesse agité."

119. Bardon, *2*, 172: "Je me proposai plutôt, si jamais je sortais de prison, d'acheter une chaumière et d'y aller vivre en philosophe."

120. The measure of Gil Blas's stability at the end is that he is flexible enough to return to the court, yet firm enough to remain internally ordered even when he becomes the assistant to the Duke of Olivarez: "I slept soundly, without being haunted by those flattering delusions which might have occupied my mind; whereas the ambitious Scipio took little rest . . ." (*3*, 290; Bardon, *2*, 282).

121. Compare Pablos' deciding to leave his good job as director of the actors' company in order to become a wooer of nuns.

NOTES TO PART THREE

1. I do not claim that the analyses of novels in this part give complete accounts of each novel. I am only interested in showing how their individual narrators, styles, and endings relate to the generalized plot, character, and sense of life I have found in all the novels. It should also be apparent that the occasional criticisms I may make of these novels are based on a criterion of coherence and are generally accepted by other scholars. Many, however, have tended to see some of the examples given here as totally incoherent and to see the picaresque novel as a kind of hodgepodge. My own impression is that each of these books is great in its way, though few of them are perfect. Each of them has a dominant tone, maintained by a variety of devices. When that tone is occasionally shattered by material inappropriate to it, I merely point out the disharmony.

2. For a discussion of the concept of "reliability" see Wayne Booth, *The Rhetoric of Fiction*.

3. See above, pp. 22-23.

4. Fabia's point of view is briefly explored at the beginning of the incident, but the picaro's point of view dominates afterward.

5. Bataillon, 126: "porque, viendo el Señor mi rabiosa y continua muerte, pienso que holgaba de matarlos por darme a mí vida."

Notes

6. Bataillon, 98: "Huelgo de contar a vuestra merced estas niñerías, para mostrar cuánta virtud sea saber los hombres subir siendo bajos. . . ."

7. Bataillon, 98: "tenía otras mil formas y maneras para sacar el dinero."

8. Bataillon, 210: "En el cual, el día de hoy, vivo y resido a servicio de Dios y de vuestra merced."

9. Bataillon, 90: "Peus, siendo yo niñu de ocho años. . . ."

10. Of course, his tale is not absolutely chaotic; then there would be no tale at all. It only has the appearance of chaos.

11. Gili, *1*, 115: "No sé qué disculpa darte, sino es la que dan los que llevan por delante sus bestias de carga, que dan con el hombre que encuentran contra una pared o le derriban por el suelo y después dicen: 'perdone.' "

12. Gili, *1*, 113: "Alejado nos hemos del camino. Volvamos a él. . . ."; "proveedores y comisarios."

13. Gili, *1*, 113: "Esto también es diferente de lo que aquí he de tratar y pide un entero libro. De mi vida trato en éste: quiero dejar las ajenas. . . ."

14. Gili, *1*, 113: "que no hay hombre cuerdo a caballo."

15. Cited by Louis Martz in *Literature and Belief: English Institute Essays, 1957*, ed. M. H. Abrams (New York, 1958), p. 154.

16. Gili, *1*, 161: "La vida del hombre, milicia es en la tierra: no hay cosa segura ni estado que permanezca, perfecto gusto ni contento verdadero; todo es fingido y vano."

17. See above, Part Two.

18. Gili, *2*, 41-42: "¿Quieres tener salud, andar alegre, sin esos achaques de que te quejas, estar contento, abundar en riquezas y sin melancolías? Toma esta regla: confiésate como para morir; cumple con la difinición de justicia, dando a cada uno lo que le toca por suyo; come de tu sudor y no del ajeno; sírvante para ello los bienes y gajes ganados limpiamente: andarás con sabor, serás dichoso y todo se te hará bien."

19. Gili, *2*, 77: "estas desórdenes en todos."

20. Gili, *2*, 115: "Que el que no sabe con sudor ganar, fácilmente se viene a perder, como verás adelante."

21. See Del Monte, *L'Itinerario*, pp. 70-74.

22. Gili, *3*, 113: "Es tan general esta contagiosa enfermedad, que no solamente los hombres la padecen, mas las aves y animales. . . . Las piedras, aun siendo piedras y sin sentido, turban el nuestro con su fingido resplandor y mienten, que no son lo que parecen. El tiempo, las ocasiones, los sentidos nos engañan. Y sobre todo, aun los más bien trazados pensamientos."

23. "La sola conclusione di un itinerario come quello di Guzmán avrebbe potuto essere l'ascetismo antisociale, non una conversione alla norma religiosa e un'adesione alla prassi sociale." Del Monte, p. 74.

24. Gili, *5,* 177: "Aquí di punto y fin a estas desgracias. Rematé la cuenta con mi mala vida. La que después gasté todo el restante della verás en la tercera y última parte, si el cielo me la diere antes de la eterna que todos esperamos."

25. Gili, *5,* 177: "como libre anduviese . . . absolutamente."

26. Gili, *1,* 36-37: "poca consideración," "teniendo claros ojos, no quieren ver, precipitados de sus falsos gustos," "ocioso tiempo que tuvo," "las calamidades y pobreza en que vino, y desatinos que hizo por no quererse reducir ni dejarse gobernar de quien podía y deseaba honrarlo."

27. Astrana, 179: "pues nunca mejora su estado quien muda solamente de lugar, y no de vida y costumbres."

28. Astrana, 117: "Murió el angélico de unos azotes que le dieron en la carcel. Sintiólo mucho mi padre (buen siglo haya), por ser tal, que robaba a todos las voluntades."

29. A. Castro, "Prologo" to his edition of *Historia de la vida del Buscón* (Paris, 1917), p. xii.

30. Astrana, 116-17.

31. Booth, p. 367.

32. Astrana, 179: "Y fuéme peor . . . pues nunca mejora su estado quien muda solamente de lugar, y no de vida y costumbres."

33. Bobertag, *1,* 142: "Also muste ich zu Pferd und inwerden, dass einem ein einzig unglückliches Stündlein aller Wolfahrt entsetzen und von allem Glück und Heil dermassen entfernen kan, dass es einem sein Lebtag nachgehet."

34. Bobertag, *1,* 294: "Es schicket sich ein Ding auf mancherley Weise, des einen Unstern kommt Staffelweiss und allgemach, und einen andern überfält das Seinige mit Hauffen. . . ."

35. Bobertag, *1,* 295: "und ich war doch nicht so ehrlich oder gottselig, dass ich Gott gedancket hätte, weil er mich aus solcher Finsternüss und Ignorantz gezogen und zu einer bessern Wissenschafft und Erkändnuss bracht, warum wolte dann mein Glück, das er mir täglich zuschickete, in die Länge haben harren können?"

36. Bobertag, *1,* 69: "Simpler durchziehet und tadelt die Leut, / sieht viel Abgötterey zu seiner Zeit."

37. Bobertag, *1,* 70: "Anstatt der auffrichtigen Meynung, die ein jedweder rechtschaffener Christ haben soll, fand ich eitel Heucheley und sonst so unzehlbare Thorheiten bey allen fleischlich gesinneten Welt-Menschen, dass ich auch zweiffelte, ob ich Christen vor mir hätte oder nicht?"

38. Bobertag, *1*, 198: "Simpler erzehlt, wie der Teuffel dem Pfaffen / Seinen Speck stilt und macht ihm viel zuschaffen"; "lustig zu hören."

39. Of course, the first-person point of view, by sympathetically identifying us with the picaro, helps to mute any inappropriate comic effect when we are exposed to the hero's anxieties in his prosperity. See p. 170; Bobertag, *1*, 220. The first-person point of view also makes the potentially comic painful in such incidents as the vomiting of the Governor of Hanau (p. 70; Bobertag, *1*, 92).

40. Bobertag, *1*, 16: "Wiewol ich nicht bin gesinnet gewesen, den friedliebenden Leser mit dieser leichtfertigen reuter Pursch in meines Knäns Hauss und Hof zuführen, weil es schlim genug darinn hergehen wird: So erfodert jedoch die Folge meiner Histori, dass ich der lieben posterität hinterlasse, was vor abscheuliche und gantz unerhörte Grausamkeiten in diesem unserm Teutschen Krieg hin und wieder verübet worden. . . ."

41. Similar references to the process of composition are found, in the English translation, on pp. 22, 73, 119, 234, 257, *et passim*. The same references are found in Bobertag, *1*, 33, 98, 115, 299; and Bobertag, *2*, 35.

42. Bobertag, *1*, 108: "welches dann alle meine Kriegsdienste seyn, die ich derselben mein Lebtag geleistet, derowegen dann ihre Feinde mich desswegen zu neiden keine Ursache haben."

43. Bobertag, *1*, 46-47: "denn Fressen und Sauffen, Hunger und Durst leiden, huren und buben, rasslen und spielen, schlemmen und demmen, morden und wieder ermordet werden, todschlagen und wieder zu tod geschlagen werden, tribuliren und wieder getrillt werden, jagen und wieder gejaget werden, ängstigen und wieder geängstiget werden. . . ." In the German, the rush of style is achieved by using verbs exclusively, rather than nouns as in the translation. Such stylistic eruptions occur frequently. See, for example, pp. 69, 88, 126, 144, *et passim* in the English translation. The corresponding pages in the German are Bobertag, *1*, 91, 117, 163-64, 186-87, *et passim*.

44. Bobertag, *2*, 187: "ob ich aber wie mein Vatter seel. biss an mein Ende darinn verharren werde, stehet dahin. Gott verleihe uns allen seine Gnade, dass wir allesamt das jenige von ihm erlangen, woran uns am meisten gelegen, nemlich ein seeliges ENDE."

45. Bobertag, *2*, 133: "zu philosophiren und mich eines gottseligen Lebens zu befleissen."

46. Bardon, *1*, 256: "Que je jugeais mal de la patronne! Le petit bossu se mêlait de magie; et, comme on avait vanté son savior à la marquise, qui se prêtait volontiers aux prestiges des charlatans, elle avait des entretiens particuliers avec lui. Il faisait voir dans le verre, montrait à tourner le sas, et révélait, pour de l'argent, tous les mystères de la cabale; ou bien, pour parler plus juste, c'était un fripon qui subsistait aux dépens

des personnes trop crédules; et l'on disait qu'il avait sous contribution plusieurs femmes de qualité."

47. She had encountered him by coincidence before; pp. 188 ff.

48. In *Aspects of the Novel,* E. M. Forster has eloquently deplored the tyranny of the closed ending for novels in general, not merely the picaresque:

> In the losing battle that the plot fights with the characters, it often takes a cowardly revenge. Nearly all novels are feeble at the end. This is because the plot requires to be wound up. Why is this necessary? Why is there not a convention which allows a novelist to stop as soon as he feels muddled or bored? Alas, he has to round things off, and usually the characters go dead while he is at work, and our final impression of them is through deadness. . . . Incidents and people that occurred at first for their own sake now have to contribute to the denouement. . . . If it was not for death and marriage I do not know how the average novelist would conclude.

Selected Bibliography

Abrams, M. H., ed. *Literature and Belief.* (*English Institute Essays, 1957.*) New York, 1958.

Alemán, Mateo. *Guzmán de Alfarache,* ed. Samuel Gili y Gaya. 5 vols. Madrid, 1942-50.

———. *The Rogue, or the Life of Guzman de Alfarache,* trans. James Mabbe, with introduction by James Fitzmaurice-Kelley. 4 vols. London, 1924.

Algren, Nelson. *The Man with the Golden Arm.* Garden City, 1949.

———. *A Walk on the Wild Side.* New York, 1956.

Alter, Robert. *The Rogue's Progress: Studies in the Picaresque Novel.* Cambridge, Mass., 1964.

Alvarez, G. E. *Le Thème de la femme dans la picaresque espagnole.* Groningen, 1955.

Anderson, George Minor. "The Use of Language and Rhetoric in Thomas Nashe's *The Unfortunate Traveller.*" Unpublished dissertation, Yale, 1961.

Auerbach, Erich. *Scenes from the Drama of European Literature: Six Essays.* New York, 1959.

Ayala, Francisco. *Experiencia e Invención* (*Ensayos sobre el escritor y su mundo*). Madrid, 1960.

Baker, Ernest A. *The History of the English Novel.* 10 vols. London, 1924-39.

Barth, John. "An Interview: 17 April 1964," *Wisconsin Studies in Contemporary Literature,* 6 (1965), 3-14.

Battaglia, Salvatore. "Letteratura picaresca," in *Enciclopedia italiana,* 27 (Rome, 1929-39), 146-48.

Bellow, Saul. *The Adventures of Augie March*. New York, 1953.

Blanco Aguinaga, Carlos. "Cervantes y la picaresca. Notas sobre dos tipos de realismo," *Nueva Revista de filología hispánica, 11* (1957), 313-42.

Booth, Wayne. *The Rhetoric of Fiction*. Chicago, 1961.

———. "The Self-Conscious Narrator in Comic Fiction before *Tristram Shandy*," *Publications of the Modern Language Association, 67* (1952), 163-85.

Bowers, F. T. "Thomas Nashe and the Picaresque Novel," *Humanistic Studies in Honor of John Calvin Metcalf*. Charlottesville, Va., 1941.

Brenan, Gerald. *The Literature of the Spanish People: From Roman Times to the Present Day*. New York, 1957.

Brown, Norman O. *Life Against Death: The Psychoanalytical Meaning of History*. New York, 1959.

Céline, Louis-Ferdinand [Louis Ferdinand Destouches]. *Death on the Installment Plan,* trans. John H. P. Marks. New York, 1947.

———. *Journey to the End of the Night,* trans. John H. P. Marks. New York, 1934.

Cervantes Saavedra, Miguel de. *The Adventures of Don Quixote,* trans. J. M. Cohen. Harmondsworth, Middlesex, 1950.

———. *Three Exemplary Novels,* trans. Samuel Putnam. New York, 1950.

Chandler, F. W. *The Literature of Roguery*. 2 vols. New York, 1907, reprinted 1958.

———. *Romances of Roguery: An Episode in the History of the Novel. Part I. The Picaresque Novel in Spain*. London, 1899.

Cook, Albert. *The Dark Voyage and the Golden Mean: A Philosophy of Comedy*. Cambridge, Mass., 1949.

———. *The Meaning of Fiction*. Detroit, 1960.

Cooper, Lane. *Aristotle on the Art of Poetry: An Amplified Version with Supplementary Illustrations*. Rev. ed. Ithaca, N. Y., 1947.

Cornford, Francis M. *The Origin of Attic Comedy*. London, 1914.

Croce, Benedetto. "*Lazarillo de Tormes,* La storia dell' 'Escudero,'" *Poesia antica e moderna, Interpretazioni*. 2d ed. rev. Bari, 1943, pp. 223-31.

Defoe, Daniel. *A Journal of the Plague Year*. London, 1927.

———. *Moll Flanders*. New York, 1949.

Del Monte, Alberto. *Itinerario del romanzo picaresco spagnolo*. Firenze, 1957.

———. *Il Romanzo picaresco*. Naples, 1957.

Donleavy, James Patrick. *The Ginger Man*. Rev. ed. New York, 1958.

Selected Bibliography

Eidson, John Olin. "Picaresque," in *Dictionary of World Literature, Criticism, Forms, Technique,* ed. Joseph T. Shipley. New rev. ed. New York, 1953, pp. 309-10.

Ellison, Ralph. *Invisible Man.* New York, 1952.

Empson, William. *English Pastoral Poetry.* New York, 1938.

Fielding, Henry. *The History of the Adventures of Joseph Andrews and of His Friend Mr. Abraham Adams.* New York, 1950.

————. *The History of Tom Jones, A Foundling.* New York, 1943.

————. *The Life of Mr. Jonathan Wild the Great.* Oxford, 1926.

Fitzmaurice-Kelley, James. *Historia de la literatura española, desde los orígenes hasta el año 1900,* trans. Adolfo Bonilla y San Martín. Madrid, 1901.

————, and William Christopher Atkinson. "Picaresque Novel," *Encyclopedia Britannica, 17* (1957), 905-7.

Flores, Angel, ed. *Masterpieces of the Spanish Golden Age,* with introduction. New York, 1957.

Forster, E. M. *Aspects of the Novel.* New York, 1927.

Fromm, Erich. *The Art of Loving.* New York, 1956.

Frye, Northrop. *The Anatomy of Criticism.* Princeton, 1957.

García López, José. "Introducción," *La Novela picaresca.* Barcelona, 1946, pp. 5-14.

Gilman, Stephen. *The Art of La Celestina.* Madison, Wis., 1956.

Gogol, Nikolai. *Dead Souls,* trans. David Magarshack. Baltimore, 1961.

Grabo, Carl. *The Technique of the Novel.* New York, 1928.

Grimmelshausen, Hans Jacob Christoffels von. *Grimmelshausens Werke.* Vols. *1* and *2: Der abentheuerliche Simplicius Simplicissimus,* ed. Felix Bobertag, Deutsche National-Litteratur, Vols. *33* and *34.* Berlin and Stuttgart, n.d.

————. *Simplicissimus the Vagabond* . . . , trans. A. T. S. Goodrick, with introduction by William Rose. London, 1924.

Guillén, Claudio. "La Disposición temporal del *Lazarillo de Tormes,*" *Hispanic Review, 25* (1957), 264-79.

————. "Toward a Definition of the Picaresque," *Proceedings of the IIIrd Congress of the International Comparative Literature Association.* The Hague, 1962, pp. 252-66.

Haan, Fonger de. *An Outline of the History of the Novela Picaresca in Spain.* The Hague, 1903.

Hamburger, Käte. *Die Logik der Dichtung.* Stuttgart, 1957.

Hayens, Kenneth C. *Grimmelshausen.* London, 1932.

Herrero, Miguel. "Nueva Interpretación de la novela picaresca," *Revista de filología española, 24* (1937), 343-63.

Hirsch, Arnold. *Bürgertum und Barock im deutschen Roman, Eine Untersuchung über die Entstehung des modernen Weltbildes.* Frankfurt am Main, 1934.

Howe, Irving. "Mass Society and Post-Modern Fiction," *Approaches to the Novel: Materials for a Poetics,* ed. Robert Scholes. San Francisco, 1961, pp. 269-87.

———. *Politics and the Novel.* New York, 1957.

Hutman, Norma Louise. "Universality and Unity in the *Lazarillo de Tormes,*" *Publications of the Modern Language Association, 76* (1961), 469-73.

Kraemer, Erik von. *Le Type du faux mendiant dans les littératures romanes depuis le moyen âge jusqu'au XVII° siècle.* Helsingfors, 1944.

Lämmert, Eberhard. *Bauformen des Erzählens.* Stuttgart, 1955.

Langer, Susanne. *Feeling and Form, A Theory of Art, Developed from Philosophy in a New Key.* New York, 1953.

Latham, Agnes M. C. "Satire on Literary Themes and Modes in Nashe's 'Unfortunate Traveller,' " *English Studies 1948.* London, 1948, pp. 85-100.

Lazarillo de Tormes, trans. Mack Hendricks Singleton, in *Masterpieces of the Spanish Golden Age,* ed. Angel Flores. New York, 1957, pp. 25-84.

Le Sage, Alain René. *Le Diable boiteux.* Paris, 1840.

———. *Histoire de Gil Blas de Santillane,* ed. Maurice Bardon. 2 vols. Paris, 1955.

———. *The History of Gil Blas of Santillana,* trans. Henri van Laun, rev. Henri Roberts. 3 vols. Philadelphia, 1898.

Lewis, R. W. B. *The Picaresque Saint: Representative Figures in Contemporary Fiction.* Philadelphia and New York, 1961.

Lubbock, Percy. *The Craft of Fiction.* New York, 1957.

McFarland, Thomas. "Antony and Octavius," *Yale Review, 48* (1959), 204-28.

McKillop, Alan Dugald. *The Early Masters of English Fiction.* Lawrence, Kansas, 1956.

Maldonado de Guevera, Francisco. "La Teoría de los géneros literarios y la constitución de la novela moderna," *Estudios dedicados a Menéndez Pidal, 3* (Madrid, 1952). 299-320.

Mann, Thomas. *Confessions of Felix Krull, Confidence Man: The Early Years,* trans. Denver Lindley. New York, 1955.

Martin, Terence. "The Unity of *Moll Flanders,*" *Modern Language Quarterly,* 22 (1961), 115-24.

May, T. E. "Good and Evil in the 'Buscon': A Survey," *Modern Language Review,* 65 (1950), 319-35.

Mendilow, A. A. *Time and the Novel.* London, 1952.

Miller, Henry. *Tropic of Cancer.* New York, 1961.

Moreno Báez, Enrique. *Lección y sentido del Guzmán de Alfarache.* Madrid, 1948.

Nashe, Thomas. *The Unfortunate Traveller,* in *Elizabethan Fiction,* ed. Robert Ashley and Edwin M. Moseley. New York, 1956, pp. 203-308.

Northup, George Tyler. *An Introduction to Spanish Literature.* 3d ed. rev. Nicholson B. Adams. Chicago, 1960.

Orwell, George. *A Collection of Essays.* Garden City, N. Y., 1954.

Pasinetti, Francesco, ed. *Filmlexikon: Piccola enciclopedia cinematografica redatta sulla base del Kleines Filmlexikon di Charles Reinert.* Milan, 1948.

Praag, J. A. van. "Sobre El Sentido del Guzmán de Alfarache," *Estudios dedicados a Menéndez Pidal,* 5 (Madrid, 1954), 283-306.

Quevedo Villegas, Francisco de. *The Life and Adventures of Don Pablos the Sharper,* trans, by "divers hands," rev. and ed. Mack Hendricks Singleton, in *Masterpieces of the Spanish Golden Age,* ed. Angel Flores. New York, 1957, pp. 85-233.

———. *La Vida del Buscón,* in *Obras completas en prosa,* ed. Luis Astrana Marín. 3d ed. Madrid, 1945, pp. 115-79.

Ramon, Michel Robert. *Nueva Interpretación del pícaro y de la novela picaresca española hecha a base de un estudio de las tres obras maestras del genero.* Ann Arbor, University Microfilms, 1957.

Reynier, Gustave. *Les Origines du roman réaliste.* Paris, 1912.

———. *Le Roman réaliste au XVIIe siècle.* Paris, 1914.

Rojas, Fernando de. *The Celestina: A Novel in Dialogue,* trans. Lesley Byrd Simpson. Berkeley, Calif., 1955.

Roland, A. "La Psicología de la novela picaresca," *Hispania,* 36 (1953), 423-26.

Scarron, Paul. *Le Roman comique,* ed. Émile Magne. Paris, 1955.

Smollett, Tobias. *The Adventures of Roderick Random,* ed. George Saintsbury. 3 vols. London, 1895.

———. *The Expedition of Humphrey Clinker.* New York, 1943.

Ticknor, George. *History of Spanish Literature.* 3 vols. New York, 1849.

Tarr, F. Courtney. "Literary and Artistic Unity in the *Lazarillo de Tormes,*" *Publications of the Modern Language Association,* 42 (1927), 404-21.

Valbuena Prat, Ángel. *Historia de la literatura española.* 3 vols. 5th ed. Barcelona, 1957.

——, ed. *La Novela picaresca española.* 3d ed. Madrid, 1956.

Van Ghent, Dorothy. *The English Novel: Form and Function.* New York, 1961.

La Vie de Lazarillo de Tormès (La Vida de Lazarillo de Tormes), trans. A. Morel-Fatio, with introduction by Marcel Bataillon. Paris, 1958.

Watt, Homer A. and William W. *A Dictionary of English Literature, Authors, Anonymous Works, Literary Terms, Versification, Chronology.* New York, 1945.

Watt, Ian. *The Rise of the Novel: Studies in Defoe, Richardson and Fielding.* Berkeley and Los Angeles, 1959.

Wellek, René. "Henry James' Literary Theory and Criticism," *American Literature, 30* (1958), 293-321.

——, and Austin Warren. *Theory of Literature.* New York, 1949.

Willis, Raymond S. "Lazarillo and the Pardoner: The Artistic Necessity of the Fifth Tractado," *Hispanic Review, 27* (1959), 267-79.

Wimsatt, W. K., Jr. *The Verbal Icon: Studies in the Meaning of Poetry.* Lexington, Ky., 1954.

——, and Cleanth Brooks. *Literary Criticism: A Short History.* New York, 1957.

Yelland, H. L., S. C. Jones, and K. S. W. Easton. *A Handbook of Literary Terms.* New York, 1950.

INDEX

NOTE: Since all of the eight novels that form the basis of this study of the picaresque are mentioned in every section of the book, they are not listed in the index as separate entries.

163

Index